POETRY

&

CONTEMPLATION

POETRY

&

CONTEMPLATION

A NEW PREFACE TO POETICS

by

G. ROSTREVOR HAMILTON

CAMBRIDGE

AT THE UNIVERSITY PRESS

1937

CAMBRIDGE
UNIVERSITY PRESS

University Printing House, Cambridge CB2 8BS, United Kingdom

Published in the United States of America by Cambridge University Press, New York

Cambridge University Press is part of the University of Cambridge.

It furthers the University's mission by disseminating knowledge in the pursuit of education, learning and research at the highest international levels of excellence.

www.cambridge.org
Information on this title: www.cambridge.org/9781107418158

First published 1937
First paperback edition 2014

A catalogue record for this publication is available from the British Library

ISBN 978-1-107-41815-8 Paperback

Cambridge University Press has no responsibility for the persistence or accuracy of URLs for external or third-party internet websites referred to in this publication, and does not guarantee that any content on such websites is, or will remain, accurate or appropriate.

CONTENTS

INTRODUCTION   *page* ix

CHAPTERS

I   Poetic Experience: The Sphere of
       Poetics   1

II   Distractions   9

III   Unconscious Experience   13

IV   The Wholeness of Experience   22

V   Wholeness and Objective Theories   29

VI   The Growth of Experience   38

VII   The Continuity of Experience   42

VIII   Analysis of Experience   52

IX   Contemplative Experience: The Aes-
       thetic Attitude   66

X   Objective Experience   77

XI   Poetic and Ordinary Experience: The
       Difference   84

XII   Poetic and Ordinary Experience: The
       Connection   98

XIII   Creation of Experience: Definition of a
       Poet   107

XIV   Reality and Facts of Mind   119

XV   Poetic Emotions   138

XVI   The Poet and Society   144

INDEX   158

INTRODUCTION

A little more than two years ago, thinking that I might perhaps take a hand at the reviewing of poetry—which I had never yet done—I set myself to consider first principles, especially in the light of current theory. To begin with, I read an interesting book, then recently published, *The Critique of Poetry*, by Mr Michael Roberts: and from that I went on to *The Principles of Literary Criticism*, by Dr I. A. Richards, a book which had been extremely influential in the ten years since its first appearance. Soon I was in the toils, fascinated and plagued by the difficulties that lurk behind the question, What is Poetry?

The *Principles* I found exceedingly stimulating. Its enquiries went deep, it was often illuminating when it touched on particular poems, and above all it was a brave attempt at systematic thinking on original lines. It seemed to be fundamentally right in the emphasis it laid on the organization, the complex harmony, of poetic experience: and it seemed, in nearly everything else, to be fundamentally wrong. It was wrong about the mind and character of poets: wrong about art and morals: wrong about the relation of poetry to life, and wrong about the place of the poet in society. And it was not only wrong. I believed—and I believe now—that it has had a definitely harmful effect, not only on poetic theory, not only on criticism, but also on the writing of poetry itself. The modern poet is self-conscious in a high degree, and his practice is much under the sway of theory.

The influence of the *Principles* has, I think, been due partly to its assumption of scientific authority, and partly to a real virtue, that of system. The need for coherent system is deeply felt nowadays. "Our young men and women", says J. L. Stocks, writing on 'The Need for a Social Philosophy', "are attracted in large and probably increasing numbers to the Marxist creed, not so much because it is adequate and theoretically unanswerable, as because it is the only coherent body of doctrine that they can find."[1] It has been pretty much the same, in the sphere of literature, with the teaching of Dr Richards.

My small book is only a preface to poetics. Anything more ambitious in scope would require more leisure, for thinking and reading and thinking, than I have. None the less, the 'preface' is ambitious in aim, for it seeks not merely to criticize the teaching of Dr Richards (and, incidentally, certain other current views) but to help towards laying a new foundation for the theory of poetry.

I would like to mention one or two books, in my slender reading, which have helped me in various ways. Among these is Mr Sturge Moore's *Armour for Aphrodite*: while radically disagreeing with the objective theory which forms part of its basis, I was constantly impressed by the pointed wisdom of its judgment. What, for a single example, could be better than this? "Every artist contracts defects and mannerisms which betray his identity—sign what he had rather not have signed, and, like the criminal's thumb-mark, help the expert to track him. Genuineness is not excellence." Next I would mention M. Charles Mauron's *Aesthetics and Psychology*, a bril-

[1] *Proceedings of the Aristotelian Society*, 1935–36, p. 17.

liant, clear and entertaining essay. Then there is Miss Joanna Field's *A Life of One's Own*, a book of unusual interest and a remarkable testimony to the value of contemplation. And I must not omit a reference to Miss E. M. Bartlett's paper 'The Determination of the Aesthetic Minimum',[1] a penetrating essay (for all its forbidding title) to which I acknowledge my debt.

But a deeper indebtedness than any is one of old standing. Although I do not accept M. Bergson's theory of intuition as a faculty opposed to the intellect, I am convinced that his doctrine of *la durée*—of time and change and freedom—is profoundly true. It has influenced not only my thought but my whole imaginative outlook. Dr Richards refers somewhere, with characteristic intolerance, to the 'dry-rot-like invasion' of Bergsonism. The many who misunderstand M. Bergson may have made his philosophy the excuse for silly and irrational views. But that philosophy is, when properly understood, a severe intellectual discipline. Clear thinking in relation to the dynamic movement of life is far more difficult than clear thinking in relation to a neat static universe, constructed by man for the convenience of his own analysis: and clear thinking is not too common, even in that easier relation.

G. R. H.

[1] *Proceedings of the Aristotelian Society*, 1934–35, pp. 113–36.

Chapter I

POETIC EXPERIENCE

The Sphere of Poetics

Many different things happen when we look at a picture, or listen to music, or read a poem. The happenings are often especially complex in the case of a poem, since the medium is that of words—words, which we use for all the debate and business of life. Poetry, more extensively than the other arts, may provide matter for discussion outside the aesthetic sphere.

We have to ask, then, What is the true subject-matter of poetics? With what particular happenings is the theory of poetry concerned?

On such questions, simple only in appearance, much thought has been expended. It has sometimes been shallow, sometimes profound. Sometimes it has been expressed in beautiful prose, and has gained thereby in persuasive power: at other times it has been veiled in oracular obscurity, which has created an impression of deep learning and significance. But the total result is disappointing, for the tangle in aesthetic matters has never been greater than it is to-day. We need to begin again from the beginning, and to advance, as best we may, without prejudice and without pretence, step by step.

First of all, let us take note of a simple truth, namely that we come to a poem, as to any work of art, with all sorts of pre-disposition: each with his own kind of sensitiveness, his own degree of culture, his own opinions and attitude to life. The different make-up of each reader

vitally affects the quality of experience which he can get
from poetry. This fact—the diversity of experience—
hardly receives proper attention. We are inclined, when
we reflect, to dismiss it as obvious, and, when we do not
reflect, to pass judgment as if it were untrue.

Most people recognize that they have a blind spot
somewhere. A particular reader, for example, may admit
that the work of Landor, with his 'guests few and select',
is in some way beyond him. He is unable, perhaps, to see
anything much in lines like these:

> *Go on, go on, and love away!*
> *Mine was, another's is, the day.*
> *Go on, go on, thou false one! now*
> *Upon his shoulder rest thy brow*
> *And look into his eyes, until*
> *Thy own, to find them colder, fill.*

But there are many poets on whose work the same reader
will be ready to pronounce, in the most final manner, This
is good and that is bad, this is beautiful, that is ugly. An
assumption slips in that his experience is the exact experience which the poem exists to give, not coloured or
limited by the mind he brings to it. He is confident that
he not only admires, but fully understands, this (shall we
say?) in Herrick:

> *Here a solemn fast we keep*
> *While all beauty lies asleep.*
> *Hushed be all things, no noise here,*
> *But the toning of a tear:*
> *Or the sigh of such as bring*
> *Cowslips for her covering.*

He declares the poem good or beautiful. But does he feel it as a pretty appeal to sentiment, or as something a little more complex? Does he merely approve of its simplicity, its compactness of form? Or does the artistry come home to him, the way, for example, in which sense and music combine to concentrate one clear note in the 'toning' of the fourth line? Does the relation between the simply quiet close and the gravely quiet opening— 'cowslips' for 'solemnity' and 'her' for 'all beauty'— enter into the effect upon him? He may be fully responsive to these and other elements, even if he does not consciously distinguish them. But in all likelihood he is not, unless he is capable of feeling the different effectiveness of Landor's scheme, where the concentration is reserved for 'colder' in the last line—a very centre-point of power, a marble index of emotion.

If the supposed reader likes the exquisite lines of Herrick for a mere prettiness and neatness, it does not occur to him that he is failing properly to experience the poem. It is all that he can do to recognize that what he dislikes, or does not like, may be beyond him: it is much more difficult to recognize that what he *does* like is beyond him, if he likes it for wrong or inadequate reasons. The indifference of most people to poetry is not what chiefly causes it to be held in light esteem. The damage is rather done by those who remain fixed in a half liking. Poetry has value for them, a genuine value: they rightly judge of their experience as a pleasure, an amenity added to life. And, so far, all is well: but they often mistake this adventitious and rather faint pleasure for an experience of poetry in its full and true quality, and so the idea is encouraged that poetry-reading is a dilettante pursuit, not anything vital or robust.

At present I am not so much concerned with this unhappy result, as with the bias that we have to guard against in the approach to poetics. Let us get rid, if we can, of the insidious, half-conscious assumption that readers who 'like' poetry have the same experience of a poem, and only part company when they judge the value of the experience. The experience itself inevitably differs —widely among readers in general, less widely among readers of sensibility and developed taste. The best that even a sensitive reader can hope to win is an experience, not the same as, but in a fairly high degree similar to, that of the poet.

Even this he cannot do all at once. For it is another plain fact, frequently ignored, that the experience occasioned by a poem is not a momentary event, abruptly begun and ended. It is a process; and, while still simplifying the truth, we may distinguish (1) preparation, (2) appreciation, (3) effects, and (4) another kind of happening—whatever its relevance—which accompanies every stage, the nervous activity of our bodies. We must briefly consider these headings, in order to answer our original question, What is the true subject-matter of poetics?

Preparation. Every reader, as I say, brings his own idiosyncrasy to the reading of a poem. And so he has to go through a process of adjustment, which may be so slight and quick as hardly to be noticeable. On the other hand, it may be slow and difficult. The metre or rhythm may rouse a critical prejudice, due to his previous reading.

Or he may find the outlook of the poet antagonistic to his own. Again, he may have to grapple with an obscure meaning, before the poem can be enjoyed. Or—and especially with some modern poetry—he may be doubtful whether the right approach is through intellectual alertness or passive surrender. Shall he, let us say, look for intellectual coherence between the successive stages of *The Waste Land*, attaching himself to one of the several guides through Mr T. S. Eliot's territory? Or is Dr I. A. Richards right in saying that such a quest is useless, that "the items are united by the accord, contrast, and interaction of their emotional effects, not by an intellectual scheme that analysis must work out"[1]?

Appreciation. We only experience a poem as fully as we can if, and when, doubts and difficulties like these have been resolved, and a sympathetic insight achieved. For the true enjoyment of poetry, like all other aesthetic experience, is free from such questioning and distraction of the intellect. It is an experience of the contemplative imagination, having a unique tranquillity, in which the elements of sense and thought and feeling actively combine. We recognize it as good in itself, and value it for its own sake.

Effects. We may also value the poem for its incidental after effects. It may reconcile us to a harsh world or, on the contrary, it may leave us with a desire for action, even revolution. It may suggest a moral ideal or illustrate a philosophy. In so far as these effects follow on a true contemplative experience, a delight in the poem in and

[1] *The Principles of Literary Criticism*, p. 290 (Appendix B).

for itself, they represent a thinning out of that experience, a return to the world of action or speculation.

Nervous Activity. At the moment it is only necessary to note that all the above happenings are accompanied by tides of activity in the nervous system, the physical response to innumerable stimuli.

In *preparation* for the enjoyment of a poem we may have to do hard thinking, and the poem may, among its after *effects*, leave us with ideas for further intellectual exercise. Again, before we reach disinterested enjoyment, the poem may rouse in us echoes of sensual appetite or moral interest, both concerned with action; or the impulse to action may follow upon the enjoyment of the poem. Poetry, indeed, is related before and after to the whole of life; all the elements of human experience, every activity of thought and desire, contribute to it and may be affected by it. But the *appreciation* of poetry, the enjoyment, the central imaginative experience, is distinct from this intellectual and practical context. It holds thought and desire in solution, but, in its own unity, it transcends them. In ideal purity, it is not concerned with thought as such (even in a philosophic poem), or with action as such (even in a dramatic poem): for thought and action have alike become objects of contemplation. This is the distinctive mark of poetic experience.

Essentially, we may say, the theory of poetry is concerned with imaginative or contemplative experience, created through a certain metrical ordering of words, and with the values of such experience. In a secondary way it is concerned with practical and intellectual activity—with life, indeed, in its infinite variety—but only as entering into the imagination. The values of poetry, as of the other arts, are distinct from those of morality, and equally from those of speculative thought: poetry, as such, is to be judged simply by the quality of imaginative experience it gives, and not by the test of moral goodness, or of truth in reference to something outside itself.

Here, then, we have given a brief definition of the sphere of poetics, a brief indication of the nature of poetry. If the outline is too hard, it can be modified as we traverse the ground in detail. But the doctrine has, I think, a general validity, and is not merely relative to this or that outlook. It will hold good, for instance, even if we adopt a materialistic view of the world, and regard the *nervous activity* of our bodies as the thing fundamentally real. For such a view may affect the quality, but not the kind, of experience we get from poetry.

Let us consider the point. If, in the name of science, we are convinced that the mind is no more than a part of the nervous system, and that the soul is a chimaera, we are condemned to a depressing view of life. Such a view, imaginatively held, is likely to have some lowering effect on the general quality of our experience—its seriousness, its tone, and especially its width; and since, as I have said, every element of human experience contributes to poetry, it is also likely to have some adverse effect on creative work. I do not wish to press this too far, remembering that there is a poetry of pessimism and despair. But I think it is generally true.

Again, a materialistic outlook must damage our ability to appreciate poems which express a religious conception of the world. True, given a serious sense of values, we can usually accept, for the sake of imaginative experience, a particular moral or religious standpoint, seriously held, with which we disagree. But the required sense of values is likely to have suffered to some extent from our materialist views; and even if, by some human or divine grace, it has not, there comes a point at which the awareness of conflict with the truth of science (as we see it) must impede acceptance of a religious attitude.

In fine, the *quality* of our poetic experience is affected— I will not say greatly affected—by the nature of our beliefs. The *kind* of our experience, on the other hand, is not affected at all, however drab our theory of the Universe. Even with an emasculated ethic and metaphysic, we should continue to create and enjoy beautiful things. The quality, alike of creation and enjoyment, would tend to deteriorate: we might slip into that decadent condition in which art confines its attention, for Art's sake, to sense-values abstracted from life. But even if poetic experience were limited to superficial and minor perfections of form, it would remain distinctive in kind, as a peculiar imaginative satisfaction created through an ordering of words, and, as such, it would still claim the special study of poetics.

Chapter II

DISTRACTIONS

Poetic experience is of value, we have seen, quite apart from the useful effects that may flow from it, and quite apart from any significance it may have in relation, e.g., to the meaning of human existence. The special task of poetics is to concentrate on this independent value. It is a difficult task, and we are liable to be distracted from it in several different ways. The ways may vary somewhat according to the view we take of mind and its relation to matter. Let us formulate three possible views, and suggest their tendencies:

(1) The material world is bound up with spirit, and has no independent meaning or existence.

(2) There are independently real worlds of mind and matter, and interaction takes place between the mind and the highly organized matter of the nervous system.

(3) The mind is merely part of the activity of the nervous system.

If we take the first view, it may tempt us to give rein to emotion. Intoxicated with the conception of a spiritual world, we may be dissatisfied with our limited experience, seeking to pass to an experience outside ours, to a wider experience, to the 'heart of the Universe'. We may be bold to claim, as English romantics have often done, that poetry, at its highest, gives us the vision of ultimate or transcendent reality. And it must be admitted that the nature of poetic experience may itself encourage us to advance such a claim: for it has a wholeness and harmony that mirror the qualities commonly attributed to the Divine, or the Absolute, or the World of Reality.

Moreover, it is often accompanied by a feeling of illumination: and, as Dr Richards warns us, we may too lightly interpret 'this feeling of a revealed significance, this attitude of readiness, acceptance and understanding' as 'actually implying knowledge'.[1] I am not ready to agree with him that the state of mind is merely 'the conscious accompaniment of our successful adjustment to life'. The poetic experience *may* be significant of a wider reality and, if it is, that significance *may* be even more important for human life than the imaginative satisfaction which the experience gives.

But the question is a proper one for philosophical enquiry, and, whatever the answer, is outside the specific range of poetics. A study of the poetic experience in itself will not be concerned with what it may, or may not, reveal of the destiny of man. Some further reference to this matter will be found in Chapter xiv.

If we take the second view—independently real worlds of mind and matter—it may reinforce the powerful influence of the notion, dear to common sense, that beauty exists in an object, whether picture or poem, apart from any experiencing mind. This 'objective' notion diverts attention from concrete experience to an abstract thing, an external object in which beauty is supposed to inhere. It tends to reduce the experience of poetry to something passive, a reflection—or, at best, a modification—in the mind of a value outside it. It encourages the idea,

[1] *P.L.C.* p. 283.

referred to in Chapter I, that different readers passively register the same experience of a poem. Worst of all, it may induce the belief that there are external rules to which works of art must conform, and by which they may be judged.

The common-sense notion, subtilized and refined, has always had its philosophic supporters. Eminent among these is Dr G. E. Moore, who advanced an objective theory—in a form, certainly, which avoids many of its harmful tendencies, including the fallacy of external rules —in his *Principia Ethica* (1903). I propose to refer to his argument, and to more recent arguments of Mr Sturge Moore, in Chapter V. The question is, of course, metaphysical: but, in a preface to poetics, it is necessary sometimes to reconnoitre the borderland of metaphysics.

Finally, if we take the third view, we may be induced to look for the source of poetic values, not so much in experience, as in the active and healthy functioning of our own part of the physical world, the body and the nervous system. If we do so, we may as well say good-bye to poetics as a distinct study, for it becomes merely a branch of physiology.

For myself, I find it more repugnant to reason to conceive of value as existing in the perfect adjustment of the organism (apart from experience), than to conceive of value as existing in the form of a picture or poem (apart from experience). A study of nervous impulses, as affected by poetry, is not a study of poetic experience. According to Dr Richards, the unconscious impulses are supreme: the quality of experience—the conscious delight in poetry—is not to be trusted. "There are plenty of ecstatic instants which are valueless; the character of consciousness at any moment is no certain sign of the excellence of the impulses from which it arises."[1]

The next chapter will be devoted to some consideration of this standpoint.

[1] *P.L.C.* p. 132.

Chapter III

UNCONSCIOUS EXPERIENCE

In writing of 'experience' I have not until now thought it necessary to say that I mean, and shall continue to mean, *conscious* experience: for that is the normal, accepted meaning. But Dr Richards, in his *Principles of Literary Criticism*, explains in a foot-note that he will use the term throughout "in a wide sense to stand for any occurrence in the mind. It is equivalent to 'mental state, or process'. The term has often unfortunate suggestions of passiveness and of consciousness, but many of the 'experiences' here referred to would ordinarily be called 'actions' and have parts which are not conscious and not accessible to introspection as important as those which are."[1] Later, he makes it clear that by 'mental events' (and therefore 'experiences') he means happenings which are sometimes *wholly* unconscious.[2]

It is necessary that, in reading the *Principles*, we should constantly bear in mind how little store is set by consciousness. The terminology does not make it easy: for men, in the ordinary way, when they talk about their minds at all, focus attention on their conscious thoughts and feelings, and so the terms available for the description of mental activity are, most of them, steeped in the suggestion of awareness. Dr Richards divides impulses into appetencies and aversions, preferring the word 'appetency' to the word 'desire', because the former avoids the implication of a consciousness which, for the

[1] *P.L.C.*, foot-note to p. 38.   [2] *Ibid.* p. 86.

most part, is absent.[1] But the inclusive word 'impulse', of which we hear far more, is certainly not free from the aura of conscious feeling or emotion. Thus it is possible to read the *Principles* without realizing how drastic is the emphasis on the unconscious. *For what is the motif running through the book? It is nothing less extreme than this— that the essential function of the arts is to increase the activity, and promote the health, of the physical, nervous system.*

The mind, according to this theory,[2] is a system of impulses. By an 'impulse' is meant, not, as the word rather suggests, the beginning of a nervous process, but the whole of such a process beginning from a stimulus and ending in an act. Some stimuli are external (from the environment), and some internal (from within the body). They do not all evoke a response, the question which of them do so depending on the nature of the interests active in us at the time. The impulse, i.e. the process effectively set up by a stimulus, seeks to have a clear, unimpeded run, issuing in action; and the appropriate action may either be overt, or incipient and 'imaginal'. A vast number and variety of impulses are always active, and, unless they are systematized, the result must be chaotic. Success for the organism lies in a reconciliation of impulses, so as to give free and full activity to as many as possible.

Mental events, either conscious or unconscious, are said to occur between the two terminal points, the stimulus and the act. The stimulus may be regarded as the *cause* of a mental event, the conscious or unconscious accompaniments of the event as its *character*, and the action in which

[1] *P.L.C.* p. 47.
[2] *Ibid.* ch. XI, 'A Sketch for a Psychology', pp. 81-91.

it issues as its *consequence*. Mental events appear to be conscious very much in the degree that the impulses involved are complex, and new or newly organized. Conscious mental events include sensations, which depend mainly on the stimuli, and emotions, which depend mainly on the internal circumstances of the organism.

What, then, is the place of pleasure? and of emotion? An impulse, according to Dr Richards, seeks after successful activity, for its own sake, and does not aim at pleasure. Pleasure is merely incidental, and is not properly to be regarded as a quality of sensation, so much as a sign of successful activity.[1] Emotions, again, are primarily signs. They are signs of 'attitudes', that is to say, of those 'imaginal and incipient activities or tendencies to action', in which—we are told—the value of poetic experience most resides. Emotions are convenient but unreliable signs of that value: and they must not be treasured for their own sake. "For it is the attitudes evoked which are the all-important part of any experience. Upon the texture and form of the attitudes involved its value depends. It is not the intensity of the conscious experience, its thrill, its pleasure or its poignancy which gives it value, but the organization of its impulses for freedom and fullness of life."[2]

On this account of nervous activity, and its supposedly inherent value, Dr Richards founds his whole view of life, in ethics no less than aesthetics. The moral ideal he sets before us is the coherent systematization of impulses, so that they may attain their maximum satisfaction. On this

[1] *P.L.C.* pp. 96–7.   [2] *Ibid.* p. 132.

corner-stone he hopes to build 'a morality which will explain, as no morality has yet explained, the place and value of the arts in human affairs'.[1] Poetry and the other arts become revealed as the handmaids of morality: their function is to communicate and diffuse moral values.

The first thing to be said about the theory is that it does not recognize, in life or in literature, any values that are specifically aesthetic. The values throughout are those of a utilitarian ethic, having as its aim, for the individual and the community, not the greatest happiness (unless it be incidentally), but the fullest and freest activity of nervous impulses—such a fullness and freedom as are said to be achieved in the poet, the eminently moral man.

Fullness and good organization are frequently commended, and similar tests may fairly be applied to the theory itself. It has, to the intellect, an attractive simplicity and coherence, but is this achieved, like the success of 'practical efficient persons' for whom we are warned to have no 'undue admiration',[2] through suppression and exclusion? Does it even begin to fit, and to cover, the full complicated facts of existence?

The doubt arises at point after point. Is psychology, or rather physiology (for the very existence of the *psyche* is scouted), so all-important that we can dispense with any independent ethic or metaphysic? Is a prudential morality enough to account for the diversity of the human drama? Is it the true object of art to communicate the values of such a morality, or of any morality? Can life, morality, art, all be dealt with in terms of the nervous system and its organization? Or are we right in suspecting that

[1] *P.L.C.* p. 58.   [2] *Ibid.* p. 59.

mysteries are explained away, in order that a more manageable residue may be explained?

The account of a mental event in terms of causation, character and consequence, a set of aspects which it has in common with material events, instead of in terms of knowing, feeling and willing, 'a trio of incomprehensible ultimates',[1] may seem to be a simplification that promises well. But we are left with a greater mystery than all, viz. how the processes of the nervous system are transformed into consciousness. No explanation is offered, but phrases are used which suggest that consciousness is merely incidental, a mental event having 'conscious accompaniments', 'conscious characters', and so on. We are not even presented with one of those admittedly wild conjectures, which Dr Richards prefers to the 'scientifically desperate belief in the soul'.[2]

Belief in the soul is no doubt desperate from a point of view which accepts the physical world as the ultimate reality, but so, surely, is the attempt to extract consciousness from neural movement: the more so, since the structure of consciousness is unlike the structure of matter as conceived by science. Indeed, the step from belief in a purely physical world to the undeniable fact of consciousness crosses a darker abyss than the step from that undeniable fact to belief in a soul. But Dr Richards is so blinded by his scientific faith, his faith in a science which he admits to be in a conjectural state, that he is unaware of any difficulty. All is delightfully clear to him. "That the mind is the nervous system, or rather a part of its activity, has long been evident, although the prevalence

[1] *P.L.C.* p. 89. [2] *Ibid.* p. 105.

among psychologists of persons with philosophic ante-
cedents has delayed the recognition of the fact in an
extraordinary fashion."[1] The dogmatic intolerance of
this pronouncement might have been learnt from extreme
religious fanaticism—*fas est et ab hoste doceri.*

For myself, I have no wish to dogmatize on the mind-
matter relationship, or even, in an essay on poetics, to
build on the foundation of any particular view. But I am
concerned with the physiological doctrine of Dr Richards,
because he uses it in such a way as to discredit the values
of conscious experience. And my first criticism is that
there are intellectual difficulties in every view of mind and
matter, and not least in his. The world of physical science
is, after all, an abstraction, and there is no warrant to
declare that it is the only real world, or even ultimately
self-subsistent and real at all. There is no such implication
in the achievements of science, and the tendency among
modern scientists is to make more modest claims. The
attitude of Dr Richards has about it something old-
fashioned, seeming like a late echo of Victorian certitude,
as when, in 1874, Professor Tyndall "gave to his presi-
dential address before the British Association the double
character of an inquest into the death of Animism and a
funeral oration over its corpse".[2]

My second criticism is this, that, even if the physiological doctrine of Dr Richards is assumed to be sound in
itself, he makes a wrong use of it for aesthetics. The case
of aesthetics differs from that of ethics. If, from a supra-
personal point of view, the main object of human life is

[1] *P.L.C.* p. 83.
[2] William McDougall, *Body and Mind*, p. 121.

a better adjustment of the unconscious nervous system, then, no doubt, it may be that there is no true *ethical* value in conscious motive—in the 'high' sense of duty, as we call it, or in the 'noble' effort of self-sacrifice. But, as I have said before, no theory of the Universe can deny *aesthetic* value to the conscious experience of poetry or the other arts: no physiology can transfer it to the unconscious nerves and mechanisms.

It seems oddly perverse to be able to enjoy poetry, and yet to look for its value outside the enjoyment. We have seen the humble place which Dr Richards assigns to pleasure and the emotions. He advises us not to trust the character of consciousness so much as the 'readiness for this or that kind of behaviour in which we find ourselves after the experience'.[1] He is no stranger to the thrill and poignancy of poetry, but his theory leads him to write as if he had a puritanical fear of such feelings. He can say of Tragedy that "the joy which is so strangely the heart of the experience is not an indication that 'all's right with the world' or that 'somewhere, somehow, there is Justice'; it is an indication that all is right here and now in the nervous system."[2]

I agree that to read poetry for the sake of pleasure, in the ordinary sense of the word, is not enough: and I think it admirably said that Tragedy (one of the few words Dr Richards distinguishes with a capital letter) is 'too great an exercise of the spirit (*sic*) to be classed among amusements or even delights'.[3] But pleasure, amusement and delight do not exhaust the states of consciousness

[1] *P.L.C.* p. 132.   [2] *Ibid.* p. 246.
[3] *Ibid.* p. 69.

which are desirable. As descriptions of our conscious experience in reading a poem or a tragedy they fall short in varying degrees. And desire for such experience is an all-sufficient motive for our reading. Satisfying imaginative experience—that is what we rightly seek: it cannot be discredited by the failure of language to provide, in one word, a closely descriptive label.

Indeed, it is fantastic to place the value of poetry in the nervous system. Assume, if you like, that some universal Necessity or Life-force is concerned with the healthy functioning of the human organism, but cares not a rap about human feelings. None the less, it is only as conscious beings that we have values of any kind, and the rightness of the nervous system can have no interest for us except as a basis for conscious well-being, conscious satisfaction, present and continued. Poetry is of value for the quality of conscious experience it gives: and the truth about that value is not to be found by examining the way in which nervous impulses work.

It may be answered, however, that Dr Richards recognizes a derivative value in the conscious satisfaction which, so to speak, reflects the orderly working of the impulses. Be it so. It remains that the quality of conscious experience is nevertheless suspect, and in part actually denied. The value of poetry, we are to believe, does not lie in the conscious experience as a whole, even for the best qualified reader: it does not lie in 'the intensity of the conscious experience, its thrill, its pleasure or its poignancy'. It lies rather in that part (if any) of the experience, and, emphatically, of its after effects, which is a sign of well-being in the nervous system—a sign of the avoidance of conflict or resolution of discord, contributing to 'freedom and fullness of life'.

We have here a confusion between the enjoyment of poetry and its after effects, between poetic experience in itself and the ordinary experience of life. But—what is worse—we also have an emptying out of experience, a whittling away of its particular quality. When we judge the value of a poem, Dr Richards would have us turn away from the intensity of our enjoyment, and attend rather to the signs of our nervous well-being, our 'readiness for this or that kind of behaviour', our 'feeling of freedom, of relief, of increased competence and sanity'.[1] These signs are abstract things: they are factors common to all sorts of aesthetic and contemplative experience, and are a poor substitute for the wholeness of our concrete feelings. The latter, it is true, are fallible guides, although they should become less so, with the unwarped development of our taste. But it is much more dangerous to reject them and consult the signs of nervous well-being. Any such groping in the abstract dark is likely to lead to every kind of intellectual distortion—self-deceit, insincerity and sham.

[1] *P.L.C.* p. 235.

Chapter IV

THE WHOLENESS OF EXPERIENCE

'Organization' is a term frequently used in the discussion of beauty, or of aesthetic quality. Art critics, for example, like to tell us, in an objective manner, of the organization of spatial relations on a canvas, while Dr Richards, and those who follow him in his neural-subjective theory, continually speak of the organization of impulses. The term is, indeed, indispensable, but the organization which concerns us is not that of an object in itself, or of nervous impulses, or of any mere abstraction; it is that of concrete, conscious experience.

Many people find it difficult to get away from the common-sense notion that beauty, or aesthetic quality, or pleasing organization, exists in a picture or even a poem objectively, i.e. apart from any experience of the picture or poem. This notion is bound up with the idea that our experience—which we can analyse for various purposes into sensations, ideas, etc.—is actually, in its concrete nature, a whole consisting of parts. Such an idea of experience is radically false: it is perhaps the most fruitful source of error in poetics, being responsible for many other fallacies as well as those of the objective theory.

The trouble is that we are so easily misled by conceptions proper only to the structure of a physical world. The way in which we look at our surroundings—our sharpening of outlines, our perception of self-contained things—has developed so as to enable us to act effectively: and with it has developed a suitable kind of language, highly external in its reference. We think, and speak, of separate objects, occupying their several positions in space; of magnitudes greater or less, of container and contained. The language answers well to our conceptions, and the conceptions are accurate enough, serving not only our practical needs, but the needs of physical science.

But what are we to think and say of our own experience, our inner life? We look on it in much the same way as on the world about us. The mind is commonly regarded as rather like an expanding suit-case, packed in greater or less quantity, from minute to minute, with sensations and ideas, images and emotions. Some of these are simple, and it seems to us that even the less simple ones, the deeper emotions, can be taken to pieces and put together again. The pieces are simple enough, and have recognized names. We are satisfied, for example, that a particular complex emotion may be resolved into curiosity, fear and desire, three distinct elements which may also be found at work in the minds of our neighbours. As for any particular tone which makes our feeling different from theirs, it seems not so much to be inherent, as to reflect a difference in external surroundings. If only other people could be placed exactly as we are, they would feel exactly as we do. Some would feel with more intensity, some with less, but it would still be the same emotion, differing not in quality but in magnitude.

This, in brief, is the sort of attitude implicit in ordinary life. It is well suited to social needs, enabling people, in a rough way, to describe and compare what they feel. Indeed it is impossible to describe an experience or a motive without giving it some fixity and precision of outline, rather like that of a clear-cut object in space. We *have* to talk as we do.

At the same time, we do not live entirely by this attitude. When we hear an impersonal account of a man's motive for some strange act, we supplement our intellectual understanding with an effort of sympathy. We try to get at something more concrete than the labels under which human passions are classified—labels which do not tell us very much more of the real nature of the motive than, for example, an identity disc tells of the character of the soldier who bears it. We do in fact penetrate some distance behind the impersonal account of motive, and behind the useful description of the circumstances which are said to have influenced the man to act as he did. Otherwise our judgments are lacking in common humanity. And this effort of sympathy is based on a knowledge of ourselves, which, however confused it may be and ill-adapted for expression in language, is far more intimate than our ordinary way of thinking and speaking allows. For, when a man is really at close quarters with himself, he does not regard that self as an embodiment of nameable qualities:

> *a puppet drawn out upon strings,*
> *Helpless, well-coloured, with a fixed and unchanging*
>   *expression*
> *(As though one said 'heartache' or 'laughter'!)*[1]

The feelings which he may talk about, as if each had a separate corner in his soul, in reality interpenetrate. His world of experience is essentially a world of qualities

[1] Conrad Aiken, *Epilogue* to *Punch: The Immortal Liar.*

interfused in a more or less close unity. It is a world to which terms of space and terms of quantity—'greater' and 'smaller', 'whole' and 'part'—do not literally apply. For, as M. Bergson says, "just in proportion as we dig below the surface and get down to the real self, do its states of consciousness cease to stand in juxtaposition and begin to permeate and melt into one another, and each to be tinged with the colouring of all the others. Thus each of us has his own way of loving and hating; and this love or this hatred reflects his whole personality. Language, however, denotes these states by the same words in every case: so that it has been able to fix only the objective and impersonal aspect of love, hate, and the thousand emotions which stir the soul."[1] Social intercourse would be barren and dreary, if we did not interpret this skeleton language in the light of that richly concrete thing, our personal experience. It is because experience is richly organized, because its elements interpenetrate, that the imaginative use of language is possible. Language, indeed, is impotent to describe, but, mediating between one personality and another, it is powerful to suggest.

The world of experience, then, is not a quantitative world: the 'content of consciousness' (to use a convenient figure, which is quite offensively spatial) never quite falls apart, and we cannot make it fall apart, as we can chemically analyse a body. If we pretend that we can, we are merely—in Coleridge's phrase—'contriving a theory of spirit by nicknaming matter'.

It can doubtless be said that terms of space and of

[1] *Time and Free Will* (tr. by F. L. Pogson from *Essai sur les Données Immédiates de la Conscience*), p. 164.

quantity, which we have no hope of avoiding, are less inappropriate to some states of mind than to others. Introspection tells us clearly enough of images and ideas which we have not fully appropriated, which seem to float upon the surface, and to be little connected with our deeper selves. The unity here is very slack. When we are more fully alive, more of ourselves coming into play, the solidarity of our inner life becomes impressive. The extent to which a passion or emotion is characteristic of us may be judged by the complexity of the elements into which it enters, and the completeness with which it permeates them.

Let me suggest an illustration from Marcel Proust. Readers of his work will remember the long and intimate analysis he gives, in *Du Côté de Chez Swann*, of the growth of Swann's passion for Odette de Crécy. When it had once taken hold of him, this man of fashion appeared to be entirely changed. "In a restaurant, or in the country, his manner was deliberately and directly the opposite of that by which, only a few days earlier, his friends would have recognized him, that manner which had seemed permanently and unalterably his own. To such an extent does passion manifest itself in us as a temporary and distinct character, which not only takes the place of our normal character but actually obliterates the signs by which that character has hitherto been discernible."[1] But if, at its first onset, the passion was isolated as a distinct character, it did not long remain so. It re-awakened in Swann the artistic perceptions and inspirations which he had enjoyed

[1] *Swann's Way* (tr. by C. K. Scott-Moncrieff from *Du Côté de Chez Swann*), vol. II, pp. 22–3.

years ago, before becoming immersed in the frivolities of
social life. And now all these inspirations bore "the
reflection, the stamp of a particular being; and during
the long hours which he now found a subtle pleasure in
spending at home, alone with his convalescent spirit, he
became gradually himself again, but himself in thraldom
to another".[1] And so again, as we learn some time after,
with his early passion for truth. "In this strange phase
of love the personality of another person becomes so
enlarged, so deepened, that the curiosity which he could
now feel aroused in himself, to know the least details of
a woman's daily occupation, was the same thirst for
knowledge with which he had once studied history."[2]
And, we are told at length, "this malady, which was
Swann's love, had so far multiplied, was so closely inter-
woven with all his habits, with all his actions, with his
thoughts, his health, his sleep, even with what he hoped
for after his death, was so entirely one with him that it
would have been impossible to wrest it away without
almost entirely destroying him; as surgeons say, his case
was past operation."[3]

Here speaks a true insight. Yet operation is exactly
what the dissecting intelligence likes. It tries to persuade
us, for example, that, even if the emotions will not always
yield to the knife, a clean cut can at least be made between
emotion and thought, sometimes one and sometimes the
other being uppermost. And it is true that, in order to
turn introspection to account, we have not only to distinguish between them but to make numerous clear-cut

---

[1] *Swann's Way*, vol. ii, p. 29.   [2] *Ibid*. p. 78.
[3] *Ibid*. pp. 126–7.

distinctions within each. But it is a mistake to regard these, in all their precision, as native to our immediate experience, or to accept them as ultimately true of life. They are necessary distinctions, for we can get nowhere without the help of analysis: but all analysis is beset with the risk of error, and especially when turned in upon the living mind. Coleridge wrote of himself that he seldom felt without thinking or thought without feeling. The activities of heart and mind were fused in him to an exceptional degree. But ordinary men may, in a dry sense, adopt his words and even go further. For, as Driesch says, "in the last resort we must never forget that a perception is also a feeling and a thought—a thought is never quite free of feeling and perceiving, etc."[1] To pursue our clear-cut distinctions too far is to defeat the aim of clear thinking.

[1] *The Crisis in Psychology*, p. 23.

Chapter V

WHOLENESS AND OBJECTIVE THEORIES

The treatment of experience as made up of separable parts, rather than of elements which interpenetrate, appears to vitiate the theory of 'organic wholes', which Dr G. E. Moore propounds, with subtle elaboration, in his *Principia Ethica*. In this theory, he explains, the term 'organic' is used in one sense only, 'to denote the fact that a whole has an intrinsic value different in amount from the sum of the values of its parts'.[1] An aesthetic experience is such a whole, and in it he distinguishes three parts, the beautiful thing itself, the consciousness of it, and the emotion appropriate to it.

To the beautiful thing in its independence he is inclined to attribute some value, although slight.[2] The consciousness entering into the whole appears to be an uncoloured awareness, for it may enter into any experience whatever.[3] The emotion, again, appears to have a free-lance character, since the *same* emotion can be directed to different objects.[4]

If, in truth, a valuable aesthetic experience were made up of such parts, the first an object of doubtful value, the second a neutral or phantom consciousness, and the third a detached emotion equally available for several contexts, it could at once be agreed that its intrinsic value was immeasurably greater than the aggregate value of its

---

[1] *Principia Ethica*, I, § 22.　　[2] *Ibid.* III, § 50 and VI, § 113.
[3] *Ibid.* I, § 18.　　　　　　　[4] *Ibid.* VI, § 114.

parts. But the intrinsic value must then be a miracle, leaving the critic of the arts with an unenviable task. He could record his appreciations in a general way, but how could he, with any confidence, dilate upon particular qualities or assign particular merits, when total value might be achieved by the alchemic union of almost valueless parts?

"The part of a valuable whole", writes Dr Moore, "retains exactly the same value when it is, as when it is not, a part of that whole."[1] And, again, the doctrine "that a part can have 'no meaning or significance apart from its whole' must be utterly rejected."[2] The doctrine, if stated in this form, may well be rejected. But the form is incorrect. An aesthetic experience is emphatically not a whole made up of separable parts. The term 'part and whole', when we are dealing with a whole the elements of which interpenetrate, does not literally apply, and is altogether misleading, unless we interpret it in the light of self-knowledge. For an aesthetic experience has the same kind of complexity as the character of an individual. Since each element of the individual's consciousness is tinged, as M. Bergson says, with the colouring of all the others, his love or his hatred reflects the whole of his personality: "there is no need to associate a number of conscious states in order to re-build the person, for the whole personality is in a single one of them."[3] Similarly, each element in our experience of a poem is tinged with the colouring of all the others. The lines would not sound to us as they do sound, were it not for the meaning, the

[1] *P.E.* I, § 19.   [2] *Ibid.* I, § 22.
[3] *Time and Free Will*, p. 165.

rhythm, the visual and tactual appeals, etc. They would
not mean to us what they do mean, except for the sound,
the rhythm, and so on. Take a Rossetti sonnet of great
technical virtuosity, *The Kiss*:

> *What smouldering senses in death's sick delay*
> *Or seizure of malign vicissitude*
> *Can rob this body of honour, or denude*
> *This soul of wedding-raiment worn to-day?*
> *For lo! even now my lady's lips did play*
> *With these my lips such consonant interlude*
> *As laurelled Orpheus longed for when he wooed*
> *The half-drawn hungering face with that last lay.*
>
> *I was a child beneath her touch,—a man*
> *When breast to breast we clung, even I and she—*
> *A spirit when her spirit looked through me,—*
> *A god when all our life-breath met to fan*
> *Our life-blood, till love's emulous ardours ran,*
> *Fire within fire, desire in deity.*

It might be said that the octet here is a ceremonious
prelude to the sestet, which contains the real theme of the
poem. But the statement, though true, would tell us very
little. It is more important to notice, for example, that
the first two lines, in the mere prose meaning of the
words, have nothing to do with the lovers' embrace; and
yet the play of vowel and consonant, and the impression
created by the words—with the violent *smouldering, sick,
seizure*—have more relevance to the embrace than to
death or disaster, suggesting in their context an almost
dizzying ecstasy of passion. This sharp excess is mo-
derated by what follows. Note, in the very marked and

deliberate verse-pattern, how the short *o* sound—*rob, body, honour, consonant, laurelled, longed for*—is prominently used, and how the labials take the lead in the stately, rather formal, movement of the lines. The whole arrangement, with the meaning felt through it, is rich and voluptuous in effect. And lastly (though many other points might be taken) note the contrast between the even progression of the octet, and the broken flow of the sestet due to the emphasis on *child, man, spirit, god*. Without this change, the sonnet would have lacked in urgency.

So we get sound, felt not purely, but through meaning, and meaning felt through sound: an ecstatic mood modified by a voluptuous, a stately movement by a broken. Whatever element we take in our experience of the sonnet reflects the character of the whole. It is just for this reason that the critic can usefully dilate upon particular qualities and assign particular merits. For—as we shall see further in Chapter VIII—whatever he may say to throw light on one of these, throws light on the whole poem.

Dr Moore's analysis of the aesthetic experience, with its attribution of independent status to the object, leads to an objective view of beauty in a somewhat extreme form, according to which beauty exists apart from all beholders. This view owes its persuasiveness to the bias of imagination. We are asked to imagine two worlds, one displaying components of extreme beauty in exquisite proportion, the other disclosing a heap of the most disgusting filth. "The one thing we are not entitled to imagine is that any human being ever has, or ever, by any possibility, *can*, live in either, can ever see and enjoy the

beauty of the one, or hate the foulness of the other."[1]
Dr Moore appeals to us whether we will not side with
him against Sidgwick in thinking it better that the
beautiful world should exist than the ugly. This is all
very well. If we whip up our imagination as we are
invited to do, we find a difficulty in straightway undoing
its work. Imagination, though not entitled to invade our
judgment, will do its best to trespass. We shall be like
children hiding their faces in their hands, but still seeing
a coveted object through cracks in their fingers.

Another exposition of objective theory is given in
Mr Sturge Moore's *Armour for Aphrodite*. "Beauty",
he writes, "is as entirely objective as light, though our
admiration of it is dependent on the integrity of our
faculties, as our perception of light is on the health of
our eyes."[2] And again, "the complete aesthetic experience includes the appearance of the admired object,
and adds to it a heterogeneous subjective complement.
As nice an organization should be achieved by this as by
the work of art itself, but one totally distinct from that,
though among its constituents is always the appearance
of the admired object."[3]

There is no more difficult matter to discuss briefly, but
I will attempt to express a differing opinion as follows:

(1) *The self-existent object*, the 'thing in itself' apart
from all beholders, which we may suppose to
exist 'behind' a work of art, cannot be said to
win any organization through the work of the
artist.

[1] *P.E.* III, § 50.   [2] *Armour for Aphrodite*, pp. 54–5.
[3] *Ibid.* p. 55.

(2) *The sensuous image or object,* which analysis separates off at the foundation of aesthetic experience, already implies a subject-object relation, and cannot simply be described as objective. Moreover, neither beauty nor fine organization can be attributed to the bare image, but only to *the aesthetic object,* that is, to the object of the developing aesthetic experience —which experience is highly subjective.

(3) With regard to *light and beauty,* neither one nor the other is objective in the sense of existing as such apart from a subject. Light is objective in the limited sense that the perception of it does not vary from one subject to another, but is common to all who have healthy sight. Beauty is not objective even in this sense, for the perception of it varies with each subject, and no common element actually exists in these various perceptions.

This statement may be developed a little under heads (1) and (2).

The self-existent object is to be distinguished clearly from the sensuous image or object. When an artist begins to work, he is using materials—his canvas and his paints —as they exist for his senses, perceived by him. The canvas, as so existing, is a sensuous object: so are the paints. But we may reasonably believe (or suppose) that, so to speak *behind* the sensuous object, there is a self-existent object of some kind, a something existing in its own right, having an inaccessible character of its own.

What is happening while the artist paints his picture?

He is altering the sensuous object, and we may suppose that, in doing so, he is in some way altering the self-existent object too.

But his whole purpose is to alter the sensuous object, the object of experience, in a way that is significant for experience. Of the self-existent object, on the other hand, he can know nothing, and any alteration which he effects in it is incidental—he does it blindly. And so he may rightly be said to be organizing the sensuous object, and to be giving it aesthetic value in the picture he is painting: but we have no warrant for saying that the blind alteration to the self-existent object has any significance, or that it implies any organization whatever.

The sensuous image or object may be taken to stand for the bare object of sense perception, as it exists for the observer with healthy sight, etc., but with no sensitiveness to art, and as it may (by a useful abstraction) be supposed to exist underlying the aesthetic appreciation of the art lover.

When I go out of a room in which I have admired a picture, I may be sufficiently assured that the self-existent object (whatever it be) remains as it was. But if I speak of the 'picture' as being in an empty room, I do not mean that it exists there independently as a sensuous image or object. For it cannot exist as such apart from relationship to a conscious subject. Whenever it does exist as a sensuous image, healthy sense-organs—to say nothing of consciousness itself—deserve a share of credit for their contribution. It is natural that the image should commonly be thought of as simply objective, for the subject seems to be entirely passive: he has only to open his eyes to see. But quite obviously the image is not objective in the sense that the subject can be ruled out.

Further, the bare image, even if objective in a limited sense, cannot have either beauty or fine organization ascribed to it. 'Beauty' is a term we should only employ for an object of aesthetic experience, for what Mr Sturge Moore calls the 'admired sensuous image' or 'admired sensuous object'. The prefix 'admired' is all-important. The gap between bare perception and admiration is due to the difference between an insensitive and a sensitive subject, and the finer the admiration, the more pronounced is the subjective element. Even if it be true that "all normal men at a certain level of development tend to admire the same objects",[1] we cannot adequately speak of beauty as objective. Beauty, rather, is to be ascribed to the object of a subject-object relation which can only come about through a fine organization of experience.

Mr Sturge Moore discriminates between the admired sensuous object and the complete aesthetic experience, which includes the appearance of that object and "adds to it a heterogeneous subjective complement". Thus the admired sensuous object or image seems to stand at some point between the bare sensuous image and the complete aesthetic object.

But it is impossible to divide the subjective organizing activity of experience into two parts, (a) a part which faithfully mirrors, with appropriate admiration, the beautiful 'appearance' of the object, and (b) a 'heterogeneous complement'. If the division were possible, experience would yield us, in (a), an objective standard

[1] *Armour for Aphrodite*, p. 17.

of beauty. But it yields no such standard, for the whole response which we make is subjective and single. The example of a re-discovered statue, admired centuries ago and still admired to-day, does point to a certain continuity of human experience, some degree of similarity (in aesthetic matters) between the mental equipment of an ancient Greek or Egyptian and that, say, of a present-day Englishman or Italian. But, in order to arrive at a common element which we may take to mirror the inherent beauty of the statue, we have to resolve the similarity between the aesthetic experience of A and that of B into identity *plus* difference, just as similarity may be resolved in the abstract world of physics or chemistry. The wholeness of experience refuses to be so anatomized. Each state of consciousness is unique. It may be more or less like other states and, for purposes of comparison and discussion, we have to analyse each state as best we can; but we are dealing with elements that interpenetrate and we can never reach a residuum of separable parts. Analysis may yield useful and fairly approximate results, but we must beware of treating the *disjecta membra* as actually existing and constituting the intact whole.

The treatment of experience as made up of separable parts is a premise with which no objective theory of beauty can dispense. And the premise is false. An organic whole does not consist of parts, and cannot be constructed with parts. It is a complex of elements not existing separately, but in a unity due to some internal animating principle. Thus aesthetic experience is an organic whole unified by a particular kind of interest, the aesthetic, the character of which will later be defined.

Chapter VI

THE GROWTH OF EXPERIENCE

We have seen that the complete aesthetic experience is a whole which cannot be divided into separate parts. The same is true of its correlative, the complete aesthetic object. Let us consider this point in relation to graphic art.

In the presence of a picture which we admire, we can, of course, withdraw to some extent the unifying power of our aesthetic interest; and, the more we do so, the less inappropriate will it be to speak of the object of our consciousness, which is losing its aesthetic character and approaching the status of a bare sensuous object, as divisible into parts. But we shall only arrive at a point where such language is exact, when abstraction has left nothing for us but a canvas filling a certain space, and we map out that space into smaller spaces, square feet or square inches. The space might better, for this exercise in geometry, be occupied by a blackboard.

Or let us suppose that, instead of merely relaxing and letting our aesthetic interest decompose, we replace it with an active intellectual interest, a curiosity, for example, as to the artist's technique, the way in which the paint has been laid on. The object of this *non-aesthetic* experience will, to a great extent, be amenable to explanation in clear-cut concepts, for that is the way in which the intelligence works. It is possible, as we shall see in Chapter VIII, to learn much about the aesthetic object through correlating it with the non-aesthetic or intellectual object. But an attempt to construct the aesthetic object out of the concepts which underlie the intellectual object would be as futile as an attempt to construct it out of the subdivisions of space underlying the canvas.

I must now pass from the complete aesthetic experience and its object to the growing aesthetic experience and the object which develops with it. Bringing in the time factor, let us ask what would happen if a picture, hitherto unknown to us, were gradually revealed, one square foot of space after another being laid bare. If we were as nearly as possible uninterested, we should be doing little more than building up a larger space by adding smaller spaces together. But, supposing our aesthetic interest to be roused in a normal degree, we should have a developing experience. In the first square foot we might admire some particular detail, scrupulously painted—a hand, a flower, an abstract form—which would impart considerable pleasure if the square were cut from the canvas and separately framed; and we might already appreciate some relation of tones, or the artist's brushwork. As square after square was uncovered, our experience would be continuously modified, and we should have a growing anticipation, increasingly but never exactly fulfilled, of the picture as it would finally appear to us, or, in subjective terms, of our final experience. That experience would certainly not represent the sum of the foregoing experiences; nor would the object, the picture as we come to experience it, represent a whole made up of parts. In the intervals between the revealing of new squares, development has taken place, and with each successive revelation there has been active new adjustment. No mere addition sum has been in progress, but what may be called a vital progression, where the whole complex of experience is continuously undergoing *qualitative* change, very different from any progression known to mathematical science.

It is the same with poetry and with music—'not a fourth sound, but a star'—as with graphic art. The vital progression (which, incidentally, is not confined to the arts, but is characteristic of all vital experience) may the more easily be realized in poetry and music, where the total experience, more obviously than in the appreciation of pictures, takes time to develop. And a poem, *as we come to experience it*, e.g. the Rossetti sonnet quoted in the last chapter, is not a whole made up of so many lines.

In poetry the mind is often shocked into surprise and the need of rapid new adjustment. Compare with any painting the visual imagery of these lines from Francis Thompson's *Ode to the Setting Sun*:

> *When thou didst, bursting from the great void's husk,*
> *Leap like a lion on the throat o' the dusk;*
> > *When the angels rose-chapleted*
> > *Sang to each other—*

The suddenness of the passing from one contrasted image to another is significant not of the time factor only, but of the ready interplay of pictures called up in the mind's eye by words. In the present context we must be content to note that, while the qualitative change marking the course of aesthetic experience cannot be measured, differences can be detected in its rapidity and profundity.

In the aesthetic experience, then, if the time factor is eliminated, what we have is a situation forming a single whole, where a particular state of consciousness and an object are involved in each other. If we substitute the dynamic approach for the static, we may consider the growth of the experience, and compare the final stage with earlier stages. The experience at each stage is a whole. At a very early stage it may be that no emotion is apparent, but at a later stage, when we say that emotion enters in, what we mean is that the whole tone of consciousness alters, not that the old state of consciousness persists, with something new and external added to it. Similarly, the final experience, which may surpass anything that has gone before, is not a larger whole, arrived at by the aggregation of smaller wholes and—as though it were a matter of space—containing them. Rather it is a closely related whole, more complex and more fully organized.

Chapter VII

THE CONTINUITY OF EXPERIENCE

It is a mistake to imagine that the earlier stages of the poetic experience fade out and leave no trace. The trace is indelible. Dr Richards, in his chapter 'The Analysis of a Poem', fails to recognize that each successive element endures (though not, of course, as a separate part) in the growing organization: that the various 'impulses' organized are none of them dying impulses, but live on, with varying force, into the unity of the completed system. This failure is shown in his treatment of imagery. According to his scheme, images are of value merely as helping to direct thought and arouse emotion, which are the fundamental things in the experience of a poem. The sensory qualities of an image—although the uninstructed reader may fancy that they hold exquisite beauty—really matter very little. So little do they matter that "images which are different in their sensory qualities may have the same effects".[1] Let us pause to consider this apparently eccentric view.

Dr Richards distinguishes

(1) 'persons of the image-producing types' and
(2) 'trustworthy people who, according to their accounts, never experience any imagery at all', but are none the less capable of art experiences.[2]

---

[1] *P.L.C.* p. 123.   [2] *Ibid.* p. 120.

Persons of the image-producing types differ, as regards the sensory aspect of their images—

    (i) in degree of vividness, delicacy, etc.;

    (ii) in the relation between the several different kinds of imagery;

    (iii) in the nature of the particular image produced within any one kind: in the free visual kind, for example, "fifty different readers will experience not one common picture but fifty different pictures".[1]

Dr Richards warns us that care should be taken "to avoid the natural tendency to suppose that the more clear and vivid an image the greater will be its efficacy"[2]— its efficacy, i.e. in directing thought and arousing emotion. Yet it seems that such a supposition as to the effects of vivid imagery would 'probably' be correct in individual cases, or that it would be so 'for many people'. For, "with persons of the image-producing types an increase in delicacy and vivacity in their imagery will probably be accompanied by increased subtlety in effects":[3] and "in all forms of imagery sensory deficiencies are for many people signs and accompaniments of defective efficacy".[4]

Notice that the greater vivacity will only be an 'accompaniment' of the greater efficacy. It will not be a cause, for what matters, and gives efficacy, is not the vivacity of the image or its "sensory *resemblance*...to the sensation which is its prototype, but some other relation, at present hidden from us in the jungles of neurology".[5]

[1] *P.L.C.* p. 122.   [2] *Ibid.* p. 120.
[3] *Ibid.* p. 120.   [4] *Ibid.* p. 123.
[5] *Ibid.* p. 120.

Thus we are asked to believe that, for persons of the image-producing types, the value of images lies in something more fundamental than their sensory quality, some mysterious relationship which controls thought and emotion: this mysterious image-relation, it is admitted, is likely to be more potent, where the images are more vivid.

What, then, of the people who never experience any imagery at all? "If certain views commonly expressed about the arts are true, by which vivid imagery is an all-important part of the experience, then these people are incapable of art experiences, a conclusion which is contrary to the facts. The views in question are overlooking the fact that *something* takes the place of vivid images in these people, and that, provided the image-substitute is efficacious, their lack of mimetic imagery is of no consequence. The efficacy required must, of course, include control over emotional as well as intellectual reactions."[1]

Thus, for the imageless, a second mysterious denizen of the jungle is called in aid, a substitute which, for the purpose of poetic experience, may have all the virtues of imagery, however vivid.

Now it is true that there are many unknown factors at the nature of which psychology can but guess. I am ready to accept that imagery, taken apart from its sensory quality, has the power in some obscure way to represent, or stand in the place of, a sensation. Further I am open to conviction on the question, still debatable, whether it is possible to think without imagery of any kind: I am even ready to assume, despite incredulity, that a few people

[1] *P.L.C.* p. 120.

exist who are devoid of imagery altogether, though it may be that they would reveal the presence of unconscious (or 'co-conscious') imagery to the hypnotist. But, so far as concerns the normal image-producing person, I have great difficulty in conceiving that the appreciation of poetry—particularly of the work of "certain great poets …remarkable for the vigour of their imagery, and dependent upon it"[1]—is not *directly*, as well as intimately, connected with the sensory quality of the individual reader's imagery. As to the abnormal few, the imageless, my difficulty is yet greater. These matters, however, are not to be decided by prejudice, and we must face the question whether there is any cogent reason to assign so low a place in the poetic experience, as Dr Richards does, to imagery in its sensory aspect.

I cannot find that there is. To begin with, the experiences of *A*, the normal reader, and *B*, the imageless reader, are known from the inside to their separate introspective selves alone. Inferential comparison between them is only possible within limits, and even then is largely a matter for conjecture. But I do not rely on this negative argument. My charge against Dr Richards is

(1) that he does not make enough allowance for the different considerations that apply to imagery in practical experience, as compared with imagery in poetic experience: and,

(2) that, in poetic experience, he makes a false cleavage between the means and the end.

To serve our practical needs, we pass lightly from one image to another. If I want a cigarette and my case is

[1] *P.L.C.* p. 120.

empty, I think of the cigarette-box and the table on which it lies. I then go to the table, and get the cigarette. There is a chain of images here, mainly visual, leading from the imagined satisfaction of smoking to the actual satisfaction. The conscious images are likely to be faint and evanescent, the whole process approaching the automatic. There is no enrichment of one image by another: the images are altogether subsidiary, and might perhaps be dispensed with. From the practical point of view, it may well be that images are, as Dr Richards is inclined to think them, 'luxury products': and this is more certainly true as regards their sensory quality.

But then, from the practical point of view, poetry itself may be considered a luxury product and, that being so, we ought not to be surprised if we find that vivid imagery is among its essential requirements. The poet of vivid imagery delights in his images and their sensory quality. He is not hurrying on to action; his objective is not action, but what may best be described as *an experience growing into completion*. So he does not discard his images by the way, but develops them in their sensory quality, so as to enrich one another and also to combine with all kinds of other elements into an intricate harmony:

> *Life is the rose's hope while yet unblown;*
> *The reading of an ever-changing tale;*
> *The light uplifting of a maiden's veil;*
> *A pigeon tumbling in clear summer air;*
> *A laughing school-boy, without grief or care,*
> *Riding the springy branches of an elm.*[1]

[1] Keats, *Sleep and Poetry*

In Keats there is a lingering on the individual images. But where the images are lightly suggested or half-developed—a feature of Meredith's poetry, justly noted by Dr Richards[1]—the sensory quality need not be of less importance.

Thus, in poetry, images do not, as they do in practical life, simply stand in the place of past sensations until they have served their turn. Rather, they appear to be an enduring element, and we must altogether disagree when Dr Richards separates the experience of them, as a means, from the experience of thoughts and emotions as an end, making the value of the poem depend on the latter. As though the means were external to the poem! Or as though, if allowed to be internal to so organic a structure, they could be dismissed as not bound up with its final value! True, a mere virtuosity in forming images (conceits that tickle the surface of thought and do not touch the emotion) is, like faith without works, of little value: the important images are those which rouse us to feel, and often to think. But the thought and emotion aroused by such images are in varying degrees permeated by their sensory quality, and that quality in its turn by the thought and emotion. There are fine poems, like Francis Thompson's *Ode to the Setting Sun* (quoted in the last chapter), which are a revel of imagery. They arouse in us emotions simply saturated with image-quality, such as nothing else in the world apart from their particular images could give.

The poetry that dwells on the further side of imagery, having cast off its delights and splendours, is rare—'the

[1] *P.L.C.* p. 124.

song some loaded poets reach at last'.[1] And there are many poems where images are sparingly used, but have a dominating power. Consider, e.g., this stanza from Donne:

As lightning, or a taper's light,
Thine eyes, and not thy noise waked me;
Yet I thought thee
—For thou lov'st truth—an angel, at first sight;
But when I saw thou saw'st my heart,
And knew'st my thoughts beyond an angel's art,
When thou knew'st what I dreamt, when thou knew'st when
Excess of joy would wake me, and camest then,
I must confess, it could not choose but be
Profane, to think thee anything but thee.

The opening imagery is supreme. And in this instance it is not likely that the visual effect would seriously differ for fifty different readers. Apart from its context, the word 'lightning' might call up for some a picture of forked lightning, for others of sheet: while some would perhaps visualize, in different degrees, a background of cloud and storm. But in this poem, *The Dream*, a sort of unearthly gentleness pervades the whole, and excludes the picture of a zigzag flash or any image of violence. The visual image, so pervaded, is of extreme beauty.

But listen to Dr Richards, on another image of the eye. "One of the greatest living critics", he writes, "praises the line:

The fringed curtains of thine eyes advance,

for the 'ravishing beauty' of the visual images excited. This common mistake of exaggerating personal accidents

---

[1] Alice Meynell, *The Courts.*

in the means by which a poem attains its end into the chief
value of the poem is due to excessive trust in the common-
places of psychology."[1] We may connect with this rebuke
the following more indulgent remarks which occur a few
pages later. "As we have seen, it is natural for those
whose imagery is vivid to suppose that vivacity and
clearness go together with power over thought and
feeling. It is the power of an image over these that is as
a rule being praised when an intelligent and sensitive
critic appears merely to be praising the picture floating
before his mind's eye."[2]

There is no justification for translating the critic in this
way. He doubtless means what he says, when he praises
the beauty of the visual image. Assume, if you like, that
some obscure image-relation of which he is unconscious
(and which no psychologist has yet tracked to its lair) is
the power that has stirred his thought and feeling: none
the less, when he introspects, he is struck by the sensory
quality of the image, affecting the whole experience. He
is wrong, of course, if he supposes that his experience—
e.g. of the line quoted—is a simple thing or purely visual.
It is exceedingly easy to make this mistake, and to overlook that the experience is highly complex and subtle,
deriving its particular 'feel' from the confluence of all
kinds of images, associations, and context suggestions.
When the critic reflects, the visual image is perhaps the
most easily recognized of all these, and its vividness is
therefore apt to obtrude overmuch: it looms larger for
introspection than it does in the experience itself. Yet—
and this is the important point—in the experience itself

[1] *P.L.C.* pp. 115–16.   [2] *Ibid.* p. 123.

it is very prominent; and it would, I think, be fair to say of the intelligent critic that what he is sometimes praising is the whole complex experience, with the visual images in the foreground—images visual still, but impregnated with suggestions that are not visual. And that is a right object for praise, even though other readers cannot experience the line or poem in exactly the same perspective or with the same emphasis. Moreover, we should not ask the critic to qualify, every time, what he says about any particular quality, by a caveat that it is only one element, and takes effect through the co-operation of other elements, indistinctly known to him. It would be intolerable if he did so, and the reader must be trusted to interpret his meaning in a particular passage in the light of his general attitude and method as a critic.

We may safely conclude that, for a reader of poetry, a general deficiency as regards vividness and delicacy of images is a serious defect: I say a 'general' deficiency, for, as indicated above, there are many different kinds of image, and those who suffer a deficiency in one kind may have a compensating strength in another.

As to the abnormal case of the imageless reader, let us assume that his image-substitutes are equal in power with images, and are capable of producing an equally strong emotional reaction. Even so, the emotion, though equal in strength, could not be the same in quality, for the emotion roused by a vivid image is imbued with its unique character. Dr Richards treats the poetic image as if it merely touched a bell and set it ringing, instead of giving, if not the whole tone, at least a particular quality of tone, to the bell's sound.

But, after all, Dr Richards is not concerned with anything so unscientific as the bell's sound. Perhaps that is his defence. He is concerned only with the *vibrations*, which may be set up by a variety of causes, one of which can be substituted for another without alteration to the effect. And the vibrations are separate and evanescent enough. We were in danger of forgetting that value does not lie in conscious experience, which holds together and endures, but in the successful activity of impulses, in the sphere of matter, in 'the instantaneous which dies and is born again endlessly'.[1]

[1] Matter at its ideal limit—see Bergson, *Creative Evolution* (tr. by Arthur Mitchell from *L'Évolution Créatrice*), p. 212.

Chapter VIII

ANALYSIS OF EXPERIENCE

The critic of poetry appears to be in a difficult position. For poetic experience holds closely together, and is a baffling object for introspection: it is organic, individual, indivisible, and it changes as it grows. How then can the critic effectively analyse it? What is he in fact doing, when he speaks of this or that, of form or content, sound or imagery, thought or emotion, *as if* the poem could be taken to pieces?

First of all let us be clear about this. No critic can fully explain a poem, for no critic can fully account to himself even for his own experience. He may find many reasons for his admiration. But the sum of those reasons, however excellent (and they may, of course, be merely deceptive), can never be commensurate with his experience, which is single and organized. And, further, the experience of a poem matures at the end of a vital process, and is what it is because of that process. The critic may get nearer to a full self-understanding, if he tries not merely to analyse his final admiration, but to recall how his admiration developed. Steps in the development, however, with the reasons appearing to operate at each step, are but separate links, and, however good the chain, can never be commensurate with the vital process, which has been continuous.

Reasons, then, being abstract, while they may throw light on the concrete experience, cannot explain it in full. The critic has to analyse: but once the wholeness of experience is broken by analysis, no synthesis can make it exactly as it was. As with Humpty Dumpty, not all the king's horses and all the king's men can avail.

The point may be brought out in another way. Although reasons that are good, and valid within their limits, can be found when we look back upon a poetic experience, they were not the *motive force* of that experience. Reasons can only be the motive force of an intellectual process ending in opinion or belief. There are plenty of critics to-day whose intellectual outfit is much too strong for their aesthetic sense. They construct clever reasons for admiring, and convince themselves of the truth of their reasons. They mistake the result of this intellectual process (which, of course, is a pleasurable exercise) for aesthetic appreciation. While sincerely believing that they admire, they are insincere in their admiration, and the lead they give has a damaging effect on the small public who genuinely want to appreciate the arts, and are genuinely dissatisfied with academic work. The self-deception spreads, for a strong aesthetic sense is a rare gift (even among this small public), while desire to be 'in the movement' is a common failing.

Even the well-balanced critic, who sets out from a real appreciation and finds good reasons to support it, will never, *merely by those reasons*, move any reader to an aesthetic experience of a poem. The reader may be persuaded into a belief that he has such an experience; but I question whether it is much better for him to think he admires a poem by Keats, when he doesn't, than to think he admires the latest fashionable absurdity, when he doesn't. The good reasons of the well-balanced critic differ from the false reasons of the one-sided intellectual in this, that they direct the attention of the reader in such a way as to assist him to develop an aesthetic experience of his own. That is the best help a critic can hope to give—and it is much.

Having thus limited the function of the critic, we must return to the problem how he arrives at his clear-cut reasons, his separate factors. It will be remembered that there is no question of relating his poetic experience to an object existing in its own right, and then taking the object to pieces. No: all his useful divisions must be marked out within experience. Three things, I suggest, make this possible:

(1) an aesthetic experience, though indivisible, has internal differentiation;

(2) a poem gives rise to other kinds of experience as well as the aesthetic, i.e. to experiences organized by what may broadly be called intellectual interest (including practical as well as speculative);

(3) the aesthetic experience can be correlated with the non-aesthetic; indeed one passes into the other, and correlation is inevitable.

In the aesthetic experience, as I said in the last chapter, a particular state of consciousness and an object are involved in each other. The intellectual experience also implies an object. Thus it is permissible to speak of correlating the aesthetic *object* with the non-aesthetic. But if we speak in such terms, we may—so strong is the inclination to externalize—forget the dependence of the object on our experience. We slip more readily into the illusory notion of an object without a subject than into that of a subject without an object. As far as possible, therefore, I prefer to use subjective terms.

Differentiation. A valuable whole, such as a poetic experience, has differentiation in a high degree. It has, so to speak, a great potential multiplicity which never becomes actual. Because of this differentiation, it is possible to focus attention, now on one aspect, now on another. All the elements usually distinguished in poetry (rhythm, vowel-music, imagery, meaning, emotion, etc.) contribute—or, more accurately, the appreciation of each contributes—to the poetic experience. The structure varies indefinitely from poem to poem: the purely sensuous elements preponderate, for example, in a poet like Ernest Dowson, while at the other extreme, as in Thomas Hardy, the sensuous resources are so sparingly used as almost to persuade us that the words are bare signs of the poet's emotion—that they, and the 'form' generally, do not much matter. Even in such extreme cases, however, the structure of experience is more complex than it seems. *My present point is that, while the elements do not exist separately for appraisal, and while each is tinged by the colouring of the rest, the critic can with some success deliberately focus his attention, so that a particular group of elements now comes into the foreground of his organization, and now recedes into the background.*

In Chapter 1, when distinguishing three stages in the experience of a poem—(1) preparation, (2) appreciation, and (3) effects—I was careful to remark that this was a simplification. In reality, one does not proceed in a straight line to a single complete appreciation, and it is a blunder to suppose that, when one first admires a poem as a whole, one has necessarily got from it the best or fullest experience of which one is capable. It may well be that we shall need many aesthetic experiences of the same poem, altering the focus of our attention for each, before we can decide which is the best total experience, or how the poem is best to be read.

Kinds of Organization. I shall continue to use the term 'poetic experience' as meaning the aesthetic experience of a poem. But a poem can be experienced in other ways as well.

Thus the critic, who has admired a sonnet, can approach it again dispassionately from the outside, or with an intellectual interest only. He can examine the rhythm alone, or the pattern of vowels and consonants. He can observe and classify the imagery, or consider the prose meaning. The experience of the critic in any one of these pursuits is organic, but the interest which organizes it is intellectual.

The critic may also approach a poem dispassionately as regards its aesthetic value, but with a keen eye to its teaching, moral tendency, or propaganda. In such a case the organizing interest of his experience will be largely practical.

What I especially want to emphasize is that we must avoid thinking of the self, or the mind, as an unchanging entity, bringing different faculties (now aesthetic, now intellectual) to bear upon an unchanging object. Rather, the mind is plastic, its organization continually changing: and this implies a continual change in its object, although in an abstract sense (which language has to follow) it remains the same poem.

The mind having this plasticity, there is no hard and fast line between the aesthetic experience and the intellectual. It is doubtful whether a *pure* aesthetic experience, without any trace of intellectual detachment, can ever be realized. However that may be, people who are capable of appreciating poetry cannot help passing from one kind of experience to the other. They pass to the intellectual kind, whenever they explicitly analyse or judge a poem. For the intellect proceeds by way of concepts, and it is only these concepts—imperfect but serviceable instruments—that make judgment possible.

Correlation. A contrast is commonly drawn, and rightly enough, between the aesthetic and the critical attitudes. But it is the sign of a thoroughly bad critic to remain fixed in a critical attitude: he is sure to be the doctrinaire person who, without knowing it, is more interested in intellectual puzzles than in poetry, and spins theories out of all relation to aesthetic experience.

The good critic is one who continually checks his analytical work by the test of experience. Analysis alters —disorganizes—the aesthetic object, and the good critic either knows it or acts as if he did. He keeps in memory, as clearly as possible, what the poem *felt* like. Not only so, but when he examines in detail the elements of the poem, he seeks to bring them into a renewed aesthetic perception. So, by a constant interchange between the concept and that perception or appreciation which is always his base, he avoids alike the application of preconceived rules, and the indulgence in tenuous refinements of logic. *This controlled analysis, which, though not commensurate with experience, has a valid relation to it, is the true task of criticism.*

So long as the critic is content to take his *total* experience of a poem, and to describe it in terms of those handy and ready-made concepts which he inherits from the work of other men, he cannot help us much. His total experience will rightly govern his estimate of the poem's importance. So far, so good: unless, however, he attends closely to the experience which he gets from different angles, he is likely to suffer from one or other of the common faults:

(1) of vagueness, the poem's value being ascribed to general qualities, equally possessed by other poems;

(2) of crudity, value being found in the emotional content of the poem, to the neglect of form, as though the emotions differed little from those of 'real life'; and

(3) of embroidery, the poem being taken as material for an imaginative construction by the critic, such as, in the rare exception, may produce a new work of art, but is not criticism proper.

Let us consider, then, what the critic can do if he approaches a poem from a particular angle, if he concentrates, say, on its sound (its auditory images). How simple a group of elements can be brought into focus as the foreground of his experience? I will quote three passages bearing on this question: the first is from the preface by Mr Arthur Symons to the *Poems* of Ernest

Dowson, while the second and third are taken from Dr Richards and from Coventry Patmore.

Ernest Dowson, so Mr Symons tells us, professed that Poe's

The viol, the violet, and the vine

was his ideal of a line of verse: and he had a theory, indicated by this preference, "that the letter 'v' was the most beautiful of the letters, and could never be brought into verse too often".

Dr Richards, on the other hand, declares that "there are no gloomy and no gay vowels or syllables, and the army of critics who have attempted to analyse the effects of passages into vowel and consonantal collocations have, in fact, been merely amusing themselves.... The way the sound is taken is much less determined by the sound itself than by the conditions into which it enters. All these anticipations form a very closely woven network and the word which can satisfy them all simultaneously may well seem triumphant. But we should not attribute to the sound alone virtues which involve so many other factors. To say this is not in the least to belittle the importance of the sound; in most cases it is the key to the effects of poetry."[1]

And, finally, Coventry Patmore addresses the 'Lady elect':

> *Give me thereby some praise of thee to tell*
> *In such a Song*
> *As may my Guide severe and glad not wrong*
> *Who never spake till thou'dst on him conferr'd*
> *The right, convincing word!*

[1] *P.L.C.* p. 137.

Grant me the steady heat
Of thought wise, splendid, sweet,
Urged by the great, rejoicing wind that rings
With draught of unseen wings,
Making each phrase, for love and for delight,
Twinkle like Sirius on a frosty night![1]

If we revert to Poe's line, it is clear, I think, that we can have aesthetic experience of it, with the sound alone in the foreground of attention: the visual images and associations in the background are not such as to startle or distract, or greatly to affect the way the sound is taken. And when our experience is organized by non-aesthetic interest, we can apprehend, in isolation, the repeated 'v'. But we cannot pass from the intellectual apprehension of the 'v' to an aesthetic appreciation. There is no such thing as a 'beautiful' consonant, or a 'gay' vowel, in isolation. So far, Dr Richards is right, and his comment has value. On the other hand, from a comparison of Poe's line with other contexts where 'v' is prominent, we may very likely agree that the letter has some special value as a component in the sound of verse: and, similarly, certain vowels or syllables, if not gay themselves, appear to be inspired with gaiety more easily than others, so that the study of 'vowel and consonantal collocations' is not a mere amusement, provided we do not ignore the other factors working with them. I find, for example, that for my own experience the sound of the word 'sun'—

For whom all winds are quiet as the sun,
All waters as the shore[2]

---

[1] *The Unknown Eros*, Book II, XVII.   [2] Swinburne, *Ave atque Vale*.

—is more apt for the expression of a subdued feeling than a joyous, and that the syllable has a definite contributory value of this kind in 'sunless'. On the other hand, the sound-effect is so delicate that it can be easily neutralized by the association of warmth and brightness. It is quite true that "we should not attribute to the sound alone virtues which involve so many other factors". But the difficult question remains: given that there is always a partnership, how much of the effect is due to the particular partner, sound?

Consider the passage from Patmore, a deliberate artist in a limited range of vowel-effects. In these exquisite lines it is hard to decide how much is due to the sound of the words, how much to the imagined sound of the wind, how much to the imagined brilliance of the night-sky, how much to the suggested immanence of triumphant thought. The rhythmical effect has also to be considered. To my feeling, the sound of the words, the pattern of syllables, is of very great importance. For the best experience of the passage, the elements in the forefront of the reader's attention must prominently include the sound.

The relative importance of the sound differs greatly according to the structure of the poem. Views like that of Dowson have no absurdity in them, so long as they are related to decadent poetry, in which there is no depth of intellectual or emotional content behind the sound to which we are attending. But in relation to complex poetry they are nonsense. We may test this by comparing an early with a late poem of Mr W. B. Yeats. In *Innisfree* we cannot but mark, as Sir A. Quiller-Couch bids us,

"how the vowels play and ring and chime and toll".[1]
And this, we conclude, goes very far to explain our
pleasure in the poem: for, apart from the visual imagery,
there is not much behind the music, and the imagery,
except in the line

> *And evening full of the linnet's wings,*

lacks subtlety. It is otherwise with *Byzantium*, e.g. with
the lines about the fabled singing-bird of metal in the
emperor's palace that

> *Planted on the star-lit golden bough,*
> *Can like the cocks of Hades crow,*
> *Or, by the moon embittered, scorn aloud*
> *In glory of changeless metal*
> *Common bird or petal*
> *And all complexities of mire or blood.*

These lines are splendid in sound, as the whole poem is.
But, however we try to concentrate on the sound, it is
difficult not to be acutely aware of passionate thought and
excited vision behind the sound and affecting it. And
indeed these qualities must be potent factors in the best
experience the poem can give.

In the appreciation of poetry, then, while no absolute
separation of the various factors is possible, there is the
widest scope for useful analysis, if it be founded on a
sensitive and many-sided response. And such a response
will be reflected by the good critic in an emphasis, a sense
of perspective and proportion, which, although it can
never claim absolute rightness, will be recognized by
good readers to be reasonable and just.

[1] *On the Art of Writing*, p. 141.

A further point calls for attention. Although the one or two quotations above are mere fragments, I have not forgotten that a whole poem forms a unit. The experience of the whole poem should have a greater value than the experience of any line or passage it contains. But this is not always so. By an ideal standard most good poems are interesting failures; the experience which they give lacks, in some way or other, the completeness and coherence of a perfect organism. Sometimes the experience of, say, three stanzas in a four-stanza lyric may be more organic than the experience of the whole; and the fault is not invariably that of the reader.

Consider the relation of a single memorable line to its context. In one case it will stand out, in contrast, from a poem of obviously inferior texture. In another it will represent a climax, one of the wave-crests in a fine poem: such a line as Rossetti's in *The Portrait*—

Loud yearned the iron-bosomed sea

—a line organic to the poem, though effecting in itself a union of opposite suggestions (yearning, loudness, iron, bosom), which dominate the splendour of sound and produce a rare wholeness of impression. Sometimes a line is valued more than it deserves, because it introduces a more sensuous note into a context of astringent virtue— like the rare smile on a face usually severe. Sometimes it will be the flash of genius seeming, in a passionate writer like Donne, to light up a poem which as a whole disdains perfection.

After all, we build up the experience of a poem as we read or hear it, line by line, and the ideal critic should seek

to discover not only the best total experience, but its
relation to the experience of passage or line. Enthusiasm
for the passage or line may result in a hasty over-valuation
of a whole that is ill-organized: and, *vice versa*, in the poem
where organization triumphs, the natural tendency is to
attribute to the passage or line an effect that really proceeds from the whole. There is an example of this in
A. Clutton-Brock's discussion[1] of Marvell's poem *To His
Coy Mistress*. "There follows", he writes, "the couplet
wonderful in sound and sense—

> *My vegetable love should grow*
> *Vaster than empires and more slow*

—a couplet that makes one think of pumpkins and
eternity in one breath, preparing for the great stroke of
the poem:

> *But at my back I always hear*
> *Time's winged chariot hurrying near*
> *And yonder all before us lie*
> *Deserts of vast eternity*."

The sound of the couplet (Dowson would have noted the
use of 'v') admirably goes with the sense. But, though
the couplet is a fit preparation, it does not by itself join
the pumpkin with eternity (a difficult association, which
that comfortable growth habitually resists at Harvest
Festival). No, it needs the succeeding lines to do that.
If the couplet alone had such force, Time's chariot and the
deserts of eternity would lose their magnificent surprise.

When we know a poem well, even the most unobtrusive
line or phrase may be remembered for a merit that seems

---

[1] *More Essays on Books*, pp. 140–2.

to be imprisoned in its few words, but is really due to our experience of it remaining steeped and immersed in our experience of the whole. It is not easy to unbuild our experience—to find our way back, when we have not noticed the route. For this reason the critical faculty should be awake and retentive from the first reading of a poem. Not only the mature experience, but the whole process, and particularly the early, incomplete impression, is of importance for critical understanding.

Chapter IX

CONTEMPLATIVE EXPERIENCE

The Aesthetic Attitude

We have seen that the central study for poetics is the nature of poetic experience in and for itself (Chapters I and II). The values of poetry lie in conscious experience. They are not to be found in the unconscious, or in the nervous system (Chapter III). Nor are they to be found in poems regarded as objects having a beauty or excellence of their own, apart from the experiencing mind. Objective theories involve the conception of experience as a whole which, even though organic, is made up of separable parts. But an organic whole does not consist of parts, and cannot be constructed with parts. Thus it is impossible, in analysing the experiences of different people—even in analysing the very similar experiences of *A*, *B* and *C* in reading a particular poem—to extricate an identical element, common to all. Experience does not provide an objective standard of beauty or aesthetic excellence (Chapters IV and V).

The elements of poetic experience interpenetrate. The experience grows, not by addition of part to part, but by qualitative inner change (Chapter VI). Since the change is organic, the earlier stages in the experience are not lost, but endure in the changing whole, as it becomes more complex and more fully organized. It is not possible, with Dr Richards, to locate the value of a poem in certain 'ends' (thought, emotion and, above all, the 'attitude' aroused), as distinct and apart from the 'means' (the various kinds of imagery employed). Physiology may separate the final physical reaction to a stimulus from earlier stages in the response, but any corresponding separation is invalid for aesthetics (Chapter VII).

While experience does not consist of separate elements, the critic can vary the focus of his attention, so that this or that aspect of a poem comes into the foreground. He can, for example, have concrete experience of a poem with the emphasis now on its sound, now on its visual imagery. And with this varying experience he can correlate the sharper abstract divisions of the judging intellect, the clear-cut 'reasons' for admiring a poem. Such reasons cannot be commensurate with the experience itself. They may, however, direct the reader's attention in such a way as to help him to develop his own experience.

Every reader is a critic. The mind is plastic, its organization continually changing, and passing to and fro between the aesthetic experience of a poem (enjoyment) and the intellectual experience (judgment). A good critic is a reader who passes to and fro effectively, alternating between the aesthetic and the critical attitude, controlling his analysis by the test of constantly renewed perception. By varying the focus of his attention, he seeks to find the best perspective for the experience of a particular poem— its interflowing elements of sound, imagery, thought and emotion. He seeks, also, to discover how the experiences of passage or line are related to the total experience: how they enrich one another, and how far they are successfully organized into a single whole (Chapter VIII).

I have laid great stress on the organic wholeness of the aesthetic experience, and of its particular species, the poetic experience: I have equally stressed the organic nature of its growth, in which the whole complex undergoes continuous qualitative change. But I have remarked that these characters are also found in all really vital experience. What is it, then, which distinguishes aesthetic experience from other kinds? It is not enough to have said, without further explanation, that it is 'imaginative' or 'contemplative'.

The quest for a special aesthetic faculty or emotion is, I think, hopeless. It is merely one symptom, among many, of the intellect's craving to anatomize. There is, however, a clearly discernible difference between the general disposition of a person pausing to admire, e.g. a natural scene or a work of art, and that of a person engaged in thought or action, speculative analysis or practical affairs. It is to the former disposition that I have attached the term 'aesthetic attitude'; and 'aesthetic experience' is the kind of experience to which this attitude leads. I propose to consider three questions:

(1) What is the aesthetic attitude?
(2) How does it arise?
(3) How does it develop?

What is the aesthetic attitude? The character of the attitude is most easily seen where it is highly developed. It may be described as the attitude of pure disinterested attention. It is partly to be defined by negation. Thus it lacks both curiosity and practical interest: it does not seek either explanations or advantages, whether the latter be selfish or otherwise. It rests delightedly in its object, which seems to gather a sometimes startling beauty and significance, and it has no ulterior end in view: it does not propose to itself either action or knowledge. I reserve the honourable name, 'contemplation', to the state of mind proper to the aesthetic attitude at a well-developed stage.

The attitude has also a positive aspect, which is essential to the process of appreciation and, still more clearly, to that of creation. In the negative aspect, a comparative lack of interest in action, together with the prevalence of fatalism, both of which tend to relieve the individual from the pressure of circumstance, may help to explain why it is that contemplation comes more naturally to Orientals than to Europeans. In the positive aspect, on the other hand, a weakness in attentive control may help to account for so much of their contemplation being sterile. Were it not for the active attention of the artist (however passive he may seem, his heart 'a drop-well of tranquillity'[1]), there would be an uncontrolled attitude of dream, giving no basis for the creative energy of imagination.

The contemplative attitude is not to be confused with that creative energy. Yet it is from a contemplative trend or habit of mind that the creative impulse arises—creating, as it fulfils itself, new objects for contemplation. The connection between the two is close as that between plant and soil: from the slack contemplative you can expect no vital creation. Thus the psycho-analysts give a most inadequate account of the artist's work, when they interpret art as a kind of day-dream in which he seeks the satisfaction of thwarted desires. The psycho-analysts, as M. Charles Mauron puts it, "believe that life has forced the artist to pause, and that in more favourable circumstances he would have acted and obtained a real happiness

[1] Francis Thompson, *Contemplation*.

instead of dreaming of it; I consider, on the contrary, that the aesthetic inhibition is spontaneous, and that its object is to savour existence instead of letting it escape".[1] It is neither from lack of energy, nor from the denial to him of a crude outlet, that the artist refrains from a life of action, and creates images.

As to the nature of the artist's control, this depends on the interests and character of the individual. Breadth and depth vary enormously. All that can be hazarded is that the greater artist, and the more catholic lover of art, are likely to be found among those whose lives preserve a fair balance between the aesthetic and other attitudes. The aesthete who abstains from the ordinary commerce of life, and from the discipline of thought, may hope thereby to save his exquisite perceptions from decay, but he will be lop-sided in character and a minor artist. Perhaps he is right, so far as his art is concerned, life so cloistered suiting a narrow capacity. But he may be doing his capacity an injustice: it may be that, with a wider cultivation of sympathies, he would bring to his creative work an attention open to more subtle and numerous impressions.

How does the aesthetic attitude arise? The attitude is often evoked by something familiar seen in an unfamiliar aspect. Suppose you are climbing a hill for the sake of exercise: you know the surrounding country, it has no novelty for you, and, maybe, you are not in the habit of paying much attention to landscape. But, from time to time on your way up, you lie back against the hill, and

---

[1] *Aesthetics and Psychology* (tr. from the French by Roger Fry and Katherine John), p. 59.

look at the country below. Tree-tops are nearer to the eye than solid trunks, and the fields take on a new pattern. Your attention is arrested: you allow your eyes to take in the scene and, as likely as not, you are astonished at its vividness. For once, you are really seeing what is presented to you.

In practical affairs we get on very well without really observing what most things look like. We should be distracted from our proper end of action, if we were in the habit of falling into contemplation of the objects about us, instead of noting just enough to enable us to identify them. We easily dispense with the aesthetic attitude, so long as we are governed by our practical interests or needs. The hungry man does not make still life studies out of the viands and fruit of a spread banquet.

Common things are usually taken for granted. A chair looks different from every angle and in every light, but we ignore its changes. We carry with us our standardized picture of an object with wooden legs of equal length, a square or circular seat, and a symmetrical back—a picture which would help us if we had to make a chair, but which interferes with our seeing it as a particular pattern, an organization of line and colour changing with our angle of vision. To see it so, we require a detachment from the prejudice of use and wont, something of the innocence which enabled Van Gogh to paint his *Yellow Chair*.

The detachment may be cultivated. An excellent example is given in a recent book, by Miss Joanna Field. "Then", she writes, "I chose a small tin mug. It was an ugly object. Nevertheless I tried to keep my thoughts fixed upon it for fifteen minutes. This time I...simply let its form imprint itself upon my mind. Slowly I became aware of a quite new knowledge. I seemed to sense what I can only call the 'physics' of that mug. Instead of merely seeing its shape and colour I felt what I described to myself as its 'stresses and strains', the pressures of its roundness and solidity and the table holding it up. This sense did not come at once and I suppose it might never have come if I had not sat still and waited. But from this few minutes' exercise on a tin mug I found a clue which eventually led me to understand what was the significance of many pictures, buildings, statues, which had before been meaningless." [1]

The aesthetic attitude can be taken towards other objects than those of sense. In every sphere of life there are times when we become disinterested, either deliberately or from force of circumstances, and attend to an object for its own sake. Thus, among the rough and ready judgments of character which serve our need in ordinary affairs, we may suddenly be brought face to face with a clear revelation of motive, fascinating us by its meanness or nobility, so that we view it for a while with a sort of artistic detachment, although some answering action is required of us: here the aesthetic attitude alternates with the practical. In other cases it may alternate with the speculative. There are those, like Mr Bertrand Russell, who find in mathematics "supreme beauty—a beauty cold and austere, like that of sculpture". [2] Again, in the course of an argument proceeding step by step towards some philosophic height, we may pause to admire an idea for

---

[1] *A Life of One's Own*, p. 91.
[2] *Mysticism and Logic*, p. 60.

itself alone, and forget to ask whether it will help us to mount higher. It has sometimes been claimed that a poetic insight or vision, going beyond the power of reason, is involved in the apprehension of philosophic truth. But I think this is due to a confusion. It is rather the case that emotional experience, as of a vision, supervenes on the apprehension, and seems to give to the apprehension itself a supra-rational quality.

There is no need to multiply examples. In nearly every context there is a chance that the aesthetic attitude may arise and lead to the admiring perception of quality. The admiring perception of ideas must enter deeply into the complex process whereby philosophic poetry is created, the admiring perception of motives into that which has its end in the creation of drama.

How does the aesthetic attitude develop? I have already remarked that we pass easily to and fro between the aesthetic attitude and the intellectual. In the approach towards a complete aesthetic or contemplative experience, two unlike processes may often be detected. First, there is a response which flows out from us with so little striving on our part, that we seem to be passively submitting ourselves to the influence of the work before us. Secondly, there is a conscious effort of critical activity, sometimes very severe, breaking in upon the aesthetic attitude: we have to think, to analyse, to compare, shifting our attention from point to point as we do in practical pursuits, before we can both understand and accept the intellectual and emotional implications of the work before us. So long as this critical activity continues, there is frequent reference backwards and forwards between ourselves and the work: there may be comparison, too, with other works, and consideration of the time and circumstances in which it, and they, were created. The flowing response, on the other hand, in which imagery, thought and emotion appear to be fused, develops serenely, and may continue to develop at a stage when the critical activity has ceased to distract us, and we have been able to give ourselves up to contemplation.

Contemplation may be qualified as admiring contemplation, but the attitude is not that of judgment, for judgment implies a present awareness of the object as distinct from the experiencing subject. Yet it holds in solution the judgment or criticism, 'This object is beautiful', or, more generally, 'The contemplation of this object yields satisfaction'. If it were not for this latent criticism (crystallized only by reflection) and for the frequent reversion to an *incipient* critical attitude, we should be less clear and conscious in our enjoyments. When we sit enthralled at the performance of a tragedy, we may withhold our applause until the fall of the curtain, and be annoyed with members of the audience who break in upon a scene by clapping an exit. This is because we do not want to exchange the contemplative for the *developed* critical attitude at such a point as to hinder the progress of the former. But contemplative experience, in anything like its ideal purity, is only intermittent. Even if we know the tragedy well, so that we can surrender ourselves to its compulsion with little distraction of the intellect, we cannot be so immersed in it as not to stand apart now and then, if but for the flash of a moment, to ask ourselves a question or pass judgment of appreciation. And these

pauses help us to realize our experience. It is the same
with any long poem. The intelligent reader of an epic has
a less purely contemplative experience than the intelligent
reader of a lyric. We may say that the experience is less
purely poetic, but it is emphatically not implied that it is
less valuable.

I have been considering the aesthetic attitude, as it may
arise at some point in the flow of our day-to-day experience. When this happens, our attention is arrested. We
escape from the forward push of action or speculation, and
no longer look to the past with an exclusive eye for those
memories which may help us in our next step. Imagery,
thought and emotion, however useless in the ordinary
sense, are allowed to flow in freely from their dark
reservoirs.

Thought for the morrow is the enemy of contemplation.
And, as we should expect, the aesthetic attitude occurs
most easily when we reflect on our yesterdays, in order
(as we fondly say) to live the past over again, and not in
order to lament our misuse of time or draw lessons for
the future: for in such reflection there is no call to action.
Aesthetic experience, then, as a product of leisure, rather
assumes the aspect of a luxury, and it is a nice point how
far Professor Lascelles Abercrombie is right in claiming
that it is "the most primitive and fundamental thing in
conscious life".[1]

Part of the difficulty is that it seems impossible for
introspection to diagnose the aesthetic attitude in its
elementary beginnings. How can we say, when we

[1] *Towards a Theory of Art*, p. 14.

examine our own nascent and fugitive attention, whether an ulterior interest lurks in the background? It is only in its fuller development that we can be sure of its nature.

It is evident, of course, that the aesthetic attitude occurs in primitive peoples, but so do many other forms of conscious attention. The question is, Which has the priority? On the one hand, the aesthetic attitude is that of attention unspecialized, not narrowed and tied down, like practical attention, by a utilitarian end or by the need of action. This consideration supports the claim to *logical* priority.

On the other hand, when consciousness first appeared in this world of conflict and co-operation, it had a practical purpose to fulfil. It illumined a world where the relations between things were primarily relations of advantage and disadvantage, and the light it threw outside this sphere was more favourable to disordered dream than to anything so ordered as art. It may be then, so far as *temporal* priority goes, that the aesthetic experience is not the most primitive and fundamental thing. Consciousness would seem to have been born in chains, and we may surmise that it was a good while before it could win any degree of liberty and become, even by flashes, disinterested.

Chapter X

OBJECTIVE EXPERIENCE

In this chapter I propose to deal with an important feature of the experience which develops from the aesthetic attitude.

All experience is objective, in the sense that it involves a relation between subject and object, between self and the present content of consciousness. In this sense the aesthetic experience, when it reaches the level of contemplation, is pre-eminently objective, inasmuch as its emphasis is all on the object. Our absorption, when we contemplate, differs from the alert attention we give to a situation where a practical decision is required: here, by contrast, the self-regarding motive is absent, and there is nothing to redirect our eyes to ourselves. It differs, again, from the attention we give, e.g. to philosophy: in the pursuit of knowledge we may be selfless, but we are interested in the object of the moment for the sake of a further object at which we aim.

Thus in aesthetic activity emphasis falls most on the object and least on the subject: in practical activity it is exactly the reverse, while in speculative activity, though there may be more emphasis on object than on subject, the main weight falls on the pursuit itself. The comparison may be roughly pictured thus:

> Í inter″ested in th‴is (*aesthetic*)
>
> ‴Í inter″ested in th́is (*practical*)
>
> Í inter‴ested in th″is (*speculative*)

Just as aesthetic interest may break in, at times, upon a practical or speculative context, so, in much bad poetry, and sometimes in good poetry, we are disturbed by the obtrusiveness of practical or speculative concern. The tone of a paean beginning "Magnificent, too, is the system of drains",[1] written by a barrister, Samuel Carter (fl. 1850), would be more suitable to an advocate in some case of *Rex* v. *The Metropolitan Sewage Co.* But it would be rash to say that poetry is incapable of transcending such a theme.

Even more interesting is the case of the practical instincts. "Our deepest instincts," writes M. Charles Mauron, "such as the sexual appetite or the desire for power, are too strong not to vibrate on the least occasion. Everything serves them as a pretext for activity. The moment a sensation can suggest, in Stendhal's phrase, 'a promise of happiness', that sensation acquires the character of a signal. Some of these signals are obvious; no one will be astonished that a naked Venus should excite a sexual emotion in the spectator, or that a patriot's soul should be stirred by the national anthem."[2]

As to the former instance, we might reply that it depends on the Venus, remembering some modern styles in which the goddess is presented. In any case, if a spectator with a genuine feeling for sculpture is, and continues to be, distracted by the appeal to sex, we may suspect the artistic merit of the work. It is the same with

[1] D. B. Wyndham Lewis and Charles Lee, *The Stuffed Owl. An Anthology of Bad Verse*, p. 197.

[2] *Aesthetics and Psychology*, p. 56.

poetry: there are endless degrees of variation in the sensual basis, and in the extent to which sensuality is transcended. The question that concerns us here is, of course, one of aesthetics, not of morality. In so far as the emotion given by a poem is ultimately sensual—as distinct from sensuous and passionate—it fails to be contemplative and fails to be poetic.

It would be easy to give examples of this aesthetic failure. We might take a frankly physical poem of the seventeenth century, or—far less healthy—one of those poems of the eighteen-nineties which sought to enlarge the subject-matter of poetry by dragging in 'the music-hall, the harlot's house, the artificial paradise of drugs and drink'.[1] The decadents, in the name of 'art for art's sake', were in conscious revolt against the intrusion of morals. Their indulgence of the senses is, for that very reason, haunted by the ghost of morality and made doubly distracting.

In fact, the disciple of pure art and the moralist may fall into very much the same snare. In *The Faerie Queene*, for example, the tale of Sir Guyon's encounter with 'two naked Damzelles' is distracting both because it is a moral tale, and also because it is sensual. Spenser gives a lovely and elaborate picture of their charms:

> *The whiles their snowy limbes, as through a vele,*
> *So through the Christall waves appeared plaine:*
> *Then suddeinly both would themselves unhele,*
> *And th'amarous sweet spoiles to greedy eyes revele.*

[1] A. J. A. Symons, Introduction to *An Anthology of 'Nineties' Verse*, p. xx.

> *As that faire Starre, the messenger of morne,*
>   *His deawy face out of the sea doth reare:*
> *Or as the* Cyprian *goddesse, newly borne*
> *Of th' Oceans fruitfull froth, did first appeare:*
> *Such seemed they, and so their yellow heare*
> *Christalline humour dropped downe apace.*
> *Whom such when* Guyon *saw, he drew him neare,*
>   *And somewhat gan relent his earnest pace,*
> *His stubborne brest gan secret pleasaunce to embrace.*

There are three stanzas more to the episode, and two of
them close in the same way, by relating the beauty of the
bathers to Guyon's kindling lust. It is lovely verse, but
it is unfairly brought back from the sensuous to the sensual,
from the aesthetic to the practical, and, because it so
alternates, it is not complete or unmixed poetry.

It is the moral that does the mischief. Compare the
Epithalamion, which is joyously innocent of such pre-
occupation:

> *Behold how goodly my faire Love does ly*
> *In proud humility;*
> *Like unto Maia, when as Iove her tooke,*
> *In Tempe, lying on the flowry gras,*
> *Twixt sleepe and wake, after she weary was,*
> *With bathing in the Acidalian brooke.*
> *Now it is night, ye damsels may be gon,*
> *And leave my love alone,*
> *And leave likewise your former lay to sing:*
> *The woods no more shal answere, nor your echo ring.*

That is not sensual—it is poetry of the delighted senses,
and poetry through and through.

It remains that the complete aesthetic experience is one of contemplation, in which we are not distracted towards the practical (whether it be by a 'promise of happiness' or an insistence on moral duty), or towards the speculative (in which term I include all sorts of humble activities of the restless intelligence). The object of contemplation is the highly complex and unified content of consciousness, which comes into being through the developing subjective attitude of the percipient. It is possible that we should look here for light on the old conflict between the subjective and objective theories of beauty. In part, it is a verbal matter. When we admire a work of art, what we directly admire is the object of our aesthetic or contemplative experience. On the other hand, when we reflect, what we recognize as the cause of our aesthetic experience is a self-existent object, which, unless we are out and out idealists, we believe to exist outside us, an object with which we are brought into blind, external contact. We cannot admire that object in itself, since it does not enter into consciousness, but we can admire the power which we conceive it to have of originating in us the aesthetic experience.

To which object of our admiration, then, shall we give the name beauty? To the object of our aesthetic experience, or to the power of the external object to beget in us that experience? Professor Ross casts his vote for the latter. "The view to which I find myself driven," he writes, "in the attempt to avoid the difficulties that beset both a purely objective and a purely subjective view, is one which identifies beauty with the *power* of producing a certain sort of experience in minds, the sort of experience which we are familiar with under such names as aesthetic enjoyment or aesthetic thrill."[1]

But surely it is far-fetched to give the name beauty to such an abstraction, and I suggest that we need not be driven to do so. Subjective theory is right in declaring that without the manifold activity of vision and emotion there is no beauty: it is right in denying beauty altogether to the object conceived as existing outside experience: but it is defective, in so far as it fails to allow great importance to the objective aspect of the experience itself. True, we may concentrate on the subjective side, and rightly emphasize the complex and harmonious organization of the mind. But we shall give a one-sided account, if we do not recognize that the complex and harmonious organization does not exist apart from an objective richness. We shall rightly say, then, that beauty does exist in the object of aesthetic experience. In the consummation of such experience we forget ourselves, the distinction between subject and object almost vanishes, we lose ourselves in the object, we enjoy (in the strictest sense of the word 'ecstasy') the ecstasy of contemplation, far from action, far from reflection, however soon they may follow: and the object we contemplate is nothing but the present riches of our consciousness. That we are so deeply, selflessly and objectively engaged is an outstanding character of the aesthetic experience, to which its value must in part be attributed.

This objective aspect of the experience is something totally distinct from the notion that beauty exists outside us. Dr Santayana attributes high importance to this

[1] *The Right and The Good*, p. 127.

'radically absurd notion', which, in spite of its absurdity, persistently colours our views. "Beauty", he writes, "is an emotional element, a pleasure of ours, which nevertheless we regard as a quality of things":[1] and this objectification he regards as the differentia of aesthetic pleasure. It seems to me, however, that the important thing for aesthetic theory is not the illusory notion of a beautiful external object; it is rather the objective aspect, in which there is no illusion, of the experience itself.

Consider what this objectivity implies. It implies a complex whole of experience, so ordered that the self is content to be absorbed in it: a whole, the delicate organization of which, however variously interpreted, has been much stressed by different schools of aesthetic theory. M. Mauron, in his admirable *Aesthetics and Psychology*, writes of aesthetic organization as yielding a pure delight of the intelligence.[2] But I think that his treatment, though illuminating, is in this respect too intellectual, too narrow. No doubt the artist's process of organizing his material is partly intellectual and is accompanied by intellectual pleasure. But the resulting organization, *the being organized*— which should delight him more—radiates through all the elements of experience, sensibility, emotion, memory, and so on. To be organized well is a primary need of life: no principle could be more universal: and, in the sphere of conscious experience, the harmonious order of our faculties goes far towards constituting our delight in art, in poetry, in tragedy—our deepest emotional satisfactions.

[1] *The Sense of Beauty*, Part I, § 10.
[2] *Aesthetics and Psychology*, p. 44.

Chapter XI

POETIC AND ORDINARY EXPERIENCE:
THE DIFFERENCE

Poetry is often asked to perform other tasks than that of pure ministry to the imagination. Let me give an example. Speaking in September 1935, at Cambridge, Sir Richard Gregory is reported in *The Times* to have complained that it could not be said that the intellectual horizon of poets generally had been extended by advances in modern science. He concluded his address with 'a strong appeal for the creation of a new school of poets of science who will employ their genius to interpret scientific truths with accuracy and charm'. Within a week Sir Francis Younghusband was writing to *The Times* to say that the Religious Drama Society was eagerly awaiting the appearance of dramas from living poets who, according to the Bishop of Chichester, were ready to use their poetic art 'under the auspices of the Church for the renewal and inspiration of their fellows'. There was no poet in sight, he complained, who would 'do for the religious drama what Shakespeare did for the more secular drama': in England there was a lack of great religious dramas, "and the supplying of that lack is one of the supreme needs of the time".

The poet, it may be supposed, like David Garrick in the picture by Reynolds between the figures of Tragedy and Comedy, ought to feel flattered by these rival, though independent, appeals from Science on the one hand and Religion on the other. But no: he will be prompted, rather, to ironical comment. Does Sir Richard really think that it can be the work of a serious creative artist 'to interpret scientific truths with accuracy and charm'? Have prose-writers proved their incompetence in the useful task of popularizing science? It is good that the intellectual horizon of the poet should be extended by science, and that scientific themes should stir his imagination. It is good also that the mind of the scientist should be enlarged and liberated by the imaginative experience which poetry offers. But let the scientist come to the poet, not for the reflection of science, but for poetry: for the spirit not of these lines, doubtless accurate, addressed to *Pholas*, a shell-fish:

> *Gracefully striate is thy shell,*
> *Transverse and longitudinal,*
> *And delicately fair;*

but rather of these:

> *Strong is the lion—like a coal*
> *His eyeball—like a bastion's mole*
> *His chest against the foes:*

The first quotation is from *Conchology*, by Sarah Hoare (published in 1831), while the second is from Christopher Smart's *Song to David*.

And now for the Religious Drama Society. Does it ask the poets for great drama, because Church people or others are athirst for poetry? I can hardly believe it. In this age when poetry is so neglected, it is all very well to complain that there is no second Shakespeare in sight. What audience of to-day, indeed, deserves such poetry as Mr T. S. Eliot has given it? Let there be gratitude for this. And, so far as the poet is being asked to supply not a poetic but a religious need, let the Society lay to heart the wisdom of A. C. Bradley. "Poetry may have also an ulterior value as a means to culture or religion; because it conveys instruction or softens the passions, or furthers a good cause. . . . So much the better: let it be valued for these reasons too. But its ulterior worth neither is nor can directly determine its poetic worth as a satisfying imaginative experience."[1]

These sentences are taken from *Poetry for Poetry's Sake*, Bradley's inaugural lecture as Professor of Poetry at Oxford in 1901. They and their immediate context were attacked, twenty years later, by Dr Richards, and I propose to consider the two sides to the argument. The debate is of central importance, raising in its widest form the question suggested by the words of Sir Richard Gregory and Sir Francis Younghusband, namely, the place of poetry in the whole scheme of things.

There are four points against which Dr Richards directs his attack, and the fourth being the key position, I will proceed to examine it first. Bradley says of poetry that "its nature is to be not a part, nor yet a copy, of the real world (as we commonly understand that phrase), but to be a world by itself, independent, complete, autonomous; and to possess it fully, you must enter that world, conform to its laws, and ignore for the time the beliefs, aims, and particular conditions which belong to you in the other world of reality."[2]

Dr Richards objects to a severance set up by this doctrine between poetry and life. Bradley anticipated

[1] *Oxford Lectures on Poetry*, pp. 4–5.   [2] *Ibid.* p. 5.

such an objection, and hoped to meet it by conceding that "there is plenty of connection between life and poetry, but it is, so to say, a connection underground . . . they have different *kinds* of existence ".[1] Dr Richards, however, protests that the so-called underground connection is all-important—"whatever there is in the poetic experience has come through it ".[2]

Let us first try to be clear what we mean by the two terms of the comparison, 'poetry' and 'life'. The first term has sometimes been used in a very wide sense; for example, as Bradley observes, the poetry which Shelley defends is "the whole creative imagination with all its products. . . . And everyone, Shelley would say, who, perceiving the beauty of an imagined virtue or deed, translates the image into a fact, is so far a poet. For all these things come from imagination."[3] Such an eccentric use of language can hardly fail to result in confusion. Fortunately it is not followed by Bradley or by Dr Richards. When they speak of poetry, they refer only to experience which we get through the written word, read silently or aloud. It does not matter for the present purpose that some of the examples given by Dr Richards are drawn from imaginative prose and not from verse.

But when this kind of experience is related to 'life', what do we mean by the second term? Bradley is explicit enough. He is comparing poetic experience with experience that is 'real' in the sense that it "touches us as beings occupying a given position in space and time, and having feelings, desires and purposes due to that position ".[4]

---

[1] *Oxford Lectures on Poetry*, p. 5.   [2] *P.L.C.* p. 78.
[3] *O.L.P.* p. 155.   [4] *Ibid.* p. 6.

Dr Richards is not so clear, using for 'life' a variety of periphrastic terms. "The world of poetry", he writes, "has in no sense any different reality from the *rest of the world*, and it has no special laws and no other-worldly peculiarities. It is made up of experiences of exactly the same kinds as *those that come to us in other ways*. Every poem, however, is a strictly limited piece of experience, a piece which breaks up more or less easily if alien elements intrude. It is more highly and more delicately organized than *ordinary experiences of the street or of the hillside*; it is fragile. Further it is communicable. It may be experienced by many different minds with only slight variations. That this should be possible is one of the conditions of its organization. It differs from *many other experiences, whose value is very similar* in this very communicability.... For these reasons we establish a severance, we draw a boundary between the poem and *what is not the poem in our experience*. But this is no severance between unlike things, but between different systems of the same activities."[1]

What is the 'life' with which Dr Richards is comparing poetry? It appears to comprise all other experience. It includes both ordinary experiences of everyday, 'of the street or of the hillside', and also many experiences outside poetry which are yet 'very similar' in value.

Now it is clear that there are many contemplative and imaginative experiences other than the poetic, but having a value in some way similar or akin. We agree that no severance can be admitted between the world of poetry and such aesthetic experiences. We agree, too, that no

[1] *P.L.C.* p. 78—italics mine.

severance can be admitted between the world of poetry and the 'rest of the world', since the rest of the world includes such experiences. All this is admirable, but it does not in any way controvert Bradley's thesis. For Bradley is contrasting the world of poetry, not with other aesthetic experience, nor with a world containing it, but with the real world that touches us practically 'as beings occupying a given position in space and time, and having feelings, desires and purposes due to that position'. If Dr Richards is to overthrow Bradley's view, he must show that poetry has no 'different reality' from 'ordinary experiences of the street or hillside'. The conflict, then, is narrowed down to this point.

Let us see what distinctions, short of a 'different reality', are allowed by Dr Richards between poetry and ordinary experience. He recognizes that here it is not simply a matter of the experience being, or not being, communicable: it goes deeper than that, for the poetic experience is 'more highly and more delicately organized'. So, he would agree, is all aesthetic experience, including such a moment in the poet's day to day life as he vividly suggests in another context. "The wheeling of the pigeons in Trafalgar Square", he writes, "may seem to have no relation to the colour of the water in the basins, or to the tones of a speaker's voice or to the drift of his remarks. A narrow field of stimulation is all that we can manage, and we overlook the rest. But the artist does not, and when he needs it, he has it at his disposal."[1] True, the civil servant or business man is not likely to register and correlate such impressions. He may be

[1] *P.L.C.* p. 185.

incapable of doing so, or, though genuinely imaginative, he may be too busy or bothered. In any case, as he returns to Whitehall or the City, his experience will probably be very different. But of what nature is the difference? For Dr Richards it is not qualitative: the higher and more delicate organization of the poetic or aesthetic experience merely means a wider field of stimulation, the successful activity of a greater number of impulses—in a word, *quantitative* superiority.

This aspect is undoubtedly of great interest, and we listen to Dr Richards, the physiologist, with due respect. The ability of the poet in Trafalgar Square to harmonize a greater number of impulse-groups than the Philistine may be taken as well established. But Bradley is concerned, let us remember, with conscious experience, which he would not dream of identifying with its physiological ground or accompaniment. What matters from his point of view is the different feeling of the two men, and feeling does not have to be deduced from the physical activity of impulses. The experience of the poet, when he falls into the aesthetic attitude (for even he can't keep it up all the time!), is comparatively rich and harmonious; his mind keeps open house to diverse impressions, welcoming them for their own sake. In the experience of the Philistine, on the other hand—or, let us say, in the ordinary experience of the street—there is a drift of vague, uncoordinated, surface impressions, with a broken undercurrent, it may be, of reflection on business problems. There is no very wide severance between the experience of the poet, and the experience to be gained by reading, for example, an ode of Keats: but between the ordinary experience of the street and the reading of an ode there is a cleavage so sharp as to suggest that Bradley may not have exaggerated in speaking of two distinct worlds. It is a contrast which I have already made familiar. For the supposed experience of the poet in Trafalgar Square, and our experience when we read an ode of Keats, are alike disinterested, proper to the contemplative or imaginative mood, while the ordinary experience is related—sometimes immediately, sometimes remotely—to personal and practical interests, looking forward, in a word, to action.

Contemplation and *action*: these, indeed, are key-words. And in comparing poetic experience with ordinary experience, we must not confine our attention to the more passive phases of the latter. We must consider ordinary situations where action is present or imminent, and particularly we must consider choice. Here again, if we search the pages of Dr Richards, we find that he recognizes certain distinctions. He recognizes that "the description or the theatrical presentation of a murder has a different effect upon us from that which would be produced by most (*sic*) actual murders if they took place before us".[1] Here, too, we must ask of what nature is the difference. For Dr Richards it is only a special case "of the general difference between experiences made up of a less and of a greater number of impulses which have to be brought into coordination with one another".[2] The need for action, e.g. where an actual murder is threatened, and with it the chance elements of the situation, affect the nature of an experience, preventing its full

[1] *P.L.C.* p. 110.   [2] *Ibid.* p. 110.

development. On the other hand, in poetic experience the working out of impulses usually goes no further than 'imaginal' action, standing to overt action, 'much as an image stands to a sensation'. We are not required to take sides and interfere with the stage presentation of murder in *Macbeth* or *The Duchess of Malfi*. Consequently, the complex elements of the response may be fully and harmoniously developed. Once again, then, the difference between the poetic experience and the ordinary experience is purely quantitative: in practical affairs "the range and complexity of the impulse-systems involved is less".[1]

Where, we may ask, do the moral values come in? Dr Richards has not forgotten them. But the basis of morality, according to his view, is simply 'the effort to attain maximum satisfaction [of impulses] through coherent systematization'.[2] The need for action hinders maximum satisfaction: it requires the adoption of some impulses, to the exclusion of others, whereas all might be harmonized, and developed together, in poetic experience. Thus it is made to appear that moral values are less completely attained in ordinary experience, where action requires a choice between discordant alternatives, than in poetic experience, with its imaginal action in which discords are reconciled. It is claimed that the experiences which the arts offer "are not incomplete; they might better be described as ordinary experiences completed":[3] and again that "they are the most formative of experiences, because in them the development and systematization of our impulses goes to the furthest lengths".[4]

[1] *P.L.C.* p. 237.   [2] *Ibid.* p. 56.
[3] *Ibid.* p. 233.   [4] *Ibid.* p. 237.

This simply will not do. Dr Richards betrays a failure to understand the sphere and nature of moral values, consistent with his repudiation, in the name of psychology, of 'ethical lumber'.[1] *For morality is eminently concerned with the question how men behave, and how they should behave, in the real or ordinary world where their personal interests, advantages, etc., are touched, as they are not touched in the arts.* The response, in the real world, is incomplete without overt action. Action may be of the crudely muscular type, e.g. in grappling with a murderer (which is presumably the right response, except in those unspecified cases where the enactment of the murder would merely affect us in the same way as a description or theatrical presentation!): or it may be less conspicuously physical, though still overt, as in a spoken or written order through which a decision becomes effective. We have to take such action, not only in order to deal with situations as they arise, but also in order to build up a character of any strength. The poetic and the moral spheres are quite distinct from each other. The poetic attitude is one of wide acceptance: it is ready and able to reconcile diverse and even opposing elements. The resulting experience is completed in a harmony which, as a rule, is not accompanied by overt action: it is formative through its complex orchestral development. On the other hand, the practical—and especially the moral—attitude is one of discrimination, with a view to rejection and choice, to 'eschew evil and follow the good'. The resulting experience is completed in overt action: and here the ruthless weeding out of impulses—the reduction

[1] *P.L.C.* p. 60.

of the orchestra—may be a source, not of weakness, but of strength. The ordinary moral experience is formative, not through acceptance, but through rejection and choice.

It is vain, then, to stress the superiority of imaginal action and to exalt the poet or other artist to a moral throne. The superiority of imaginal action is valid, within limits, in the aesthetic and intellectual spheres. Our response to a play, for example, should not be like that of the audience watching a duel in Daumier's vivid and caustic painting *Le Drame*. One of the duellists has fallen, light streams on the distracted woman who has doubtless caused his death, and the mob of spectators with their scowling and passionate faces look as though they would storm the stage.

But, in the distinctively moral sphere, imaginal action is not enough. Let me quote that refreshing psychologist who can never be quite out of date, William James. "There is", he roundly declares, "no more contemptible type of human character than that of the nerveless sentimentalist and dreamer, who spends his life in a weltering sea of sensibility and emotion, but who never does a manly concrete deed. Rousseau, inflaming all the mothers of France, by his eloquence, to follow Nature and nurse their babies themselves, while he sends his own children to the foundling hospital, is the classical example of what I mean."[1] Rousseau, in short, was content in this instance with imaginal action.

The poet, or other artist, can achieve in his creative work a satisfying harmony both for himself and, in different degrees, for those who appreciate his work.

[1] *Principles of Psychology*, vol. I, p. 125.

But it is a confusion of thought to locate the highest moral value in such a harmony, however many elements or impulses it may reconcile. The man who can attain it, in the degree that an artist can, is the less likely to be impelled to seek balance and satisfaction elsewhere, in the active pursuance of a moral or religious ideal. The individual artist may be a model of virtue. But much sickening cant is talked, in a general way, about the moral superiority of the artist, or (where his behaviour makes that thesis difficult to maintain) of his superiority to morals.

I have admitted that in ordinary experience the 'range and complexity' of elements is less than in poetic experience: at the same time I have contended that this comparative narrowness or simplicity may itself be a condition of moral effectiveness and strength. This moral effectiveness is not explained by Dr Richards, who regards the basis of morality as the satisfaction of the greatest possible complex of impulses. Nor does Dr Richards explain the quality and strength of *feeling* in ordinary experience. Things that affect us 'as beings occupying a given position in space and time' come home to us differently from the contemplative experience of poetry. The poetic experience has less of what Bradley calls 'mass': more clarity, but less violence. As Miss E. M. Bartlett has expressed it, " the cutting off of emotion from its natural expression in action does not in this case, as when it is baulked of its goal by outward opposition, result in a piling-up of tension, but leads to a different *way* of feeling, which is at the same time both weaker and clearer. It may be expressed as knowing what it is to feel anger or fear rather than being actually moved by the one or the other."[1] This is well said. The poetic and the ordinary experience are characterized by different *ways* of feeling, or, as Bradley puts it, poetry and life have 'different *kinds* of existence'. In life we are angry or afraid. In poetry we have a sympathetic knowing of what it is to feel anger or fear: or, as I would prefer to formulate it, we feel these emotions (and are moved by them) imaginatively.

It is the same sort of difference as between image and sensation. We may be imaginatively moved by the remembrance of that which moved us actually on a past occasion. Dr Richards gives the following as an example of the 'increased richness and fullness in consciousness' with which new conditions may invest the familiar. "Instead of seeing a tree we see something in a picture which may have similar effects upon us but is *not* a tree. The tree impulses which are aroused have to adjust themselves to their new setting of other impulses due to our awareness that it is a *picture* which we are looking at."[2] Let us apply the illustration to the case of Horace. Horace, no doubt, was extremely frightened when his tree nearly fell on him—he was actually moved by fear. When, however, the sensation of alarm gave place to an image in memory, the tree impulses were ready to combine with others in the evolution of an ode:

> *me truncus illapsus cerebro*
> > *sustulerat, nisi Faunus ictum*
> *dextra levasset, Mercurialium*
> *custos virorum.*[3]

---

[1] *Proceedings of the Aristotelian Society*, 1934–35, p. 125.
[2] *P.L.C.* p. 110.   [3] *Odes*, ii, 17.

Here we have—what is all-important to Dr Richards—a greater quantity of impulses, giving, as a mere incident, fuller consciousness. But surely we also have something of greater moment, something qualitative, a different *way* of feeling; a way of feeling so different as to illustrate, no less effectively than more solemn examples, the contrast in kind between poetry and life, when by 'life' is meant ordinary—real, as distinct from imaginative—experience.

Chapter XII

POETIC AND ORDINARY EXPERIENCE: THE CONNECTION

So far, I think, Bradley's doctrine stands the test of criticism. But, while we have confirmed the existence of a qualitative contrast between poetic experience and ordinary experience, we have yet to vindicate the description of the two worlds as having no more than an 'underground' connection. There is such a thing as didactic poetry, with moral lessons; and again, satirical poetry, often intended to inflict personal wounds. To which world do these belong? Is it possible that the distinction between these worlds is too abstract—that they are, in fact, closely intermingled, not only in special classes of poetry, but in every kind?

In order to answer this question, we may consider the first three points in Bradley's exposition which are attacked by Dr Richards. The passage containing them is as follows:

"What then does the formula 'Poetry for Poetry's Sake' tell us about this experience? It says, as I understand it, these things. First, this experience is an end in itself, is worth having on its own account, has an intrinsic value. Next, its *poetic* value is this intrinsic worth alone. Poetry may have also an ulterior value as a means to culture and religion; because it conveys instruction or softens the passions, or furthers a good cause; because it brings the poet fame, or money, or a quiet conscience. So much the better: let it be valued for these reasons too.

But its ulterior worth neither is nor can directly determine its poetic worth as a satisfying imaginative experience; and this is to be judged entirely from within.... The consideration of ulterior ends, whether by the poet in the act of composing or by the reader in the act of experiencing, tends to lower poetic value. It does so because it tends to change the nature of poetry by taking it out of its own atmosphere.''[1]

The first of the points taken by Dr Richards as 'well worth close consideration' relates to the examples of ulterior ends. It is 'certain', he tells us, that the relation of culture, religion, instruction, etc., to the poetic experience is quite different from that of the poet's fame, etc. It is not only certain, it is obvious, and we cannot suppose that Bradley was unaware of it. But they are, all of them, possible ulterior ends, and in Bradley's view they are all alike in this one negative respect, that none of them can directly determine the *poetic* value of poetry 'as a satisfying imaginative experience'. In Dr Richards' view some of them, culture, religion, instruction, etc., 'may be directly concerned in our judgments of the *poetic* values of experiences', while the poet's fame, etc., are irrelevant.[2] A difference of view emerges—that is all. Dr Richards is mistaken if (as seems to be the case) he is suggesting for our 'close consideration' that Bradley's examples betray confusion of thought.

The second point taken against Bradley is that, as a rule, we judge imaginative experience not 'entirely from within', but from outside the experience, "by memory or by other residual effects, which we learn to be good

---

[1] *Oxford Lectures on Poetry*, pp. 4–5.   [2] *P.L.C.* pp. 74–5.

indices to its value. If by judging it in the experience we mean merely while these residual effects are fresh, we may agree."[1] It seems plain that this is far from being all that Bradley means. He means, surely, that the experience is to be judged *as from within*. Analysis inevitably breaks up the wholeness of experience. The experience is to be judged as far as possible in its un-analysed wholeness, which the critic must attempt to recapture in memory, no doubt while his memory is fresh. And if the value of one experience is to be compared with that of another, it should be by reference to the whole feeling of each in consciousness.

Dr Richards goes on to say that, in judging the experience while its residual effects are fresh, we cannot evaluate it without taking into account its place in life 'and with it innumerable ulterior worths'.[2] The truth of this assertion is by no means self-evident. Rather it depends on our general point of view; certainly, if we agree with Dr Richards that the difference between the imaginative experience of poetry and ordinary experience can be wholly resolved into a difference in the quantity of impulses engaged, we shall add up all the ulterior worths we can in our valuation of poetry; if, on the other hand, we hold with Bradley that the difference between the two experiences is a difference in kind, we shall judge the poetic worth of poetry as from within, and in scrupu-lous isolation from the effects, good or bad, that may be carried over from it into ordinary life.

"The third point"—it is desirable here to quote at greater length—"arises with regard to Dr Bradley's

[1] *P.L.C.* p. 75.   [2] *Ibid.* p. 75.

third position, that the consideration of ulterior ends, whether by the poet in the act of composing, or by the reader in the act of experiencing, tends to lower poetic value. Here all depends upon *which are the ulterior ends in question*, and what the kind of poetry. It will not be denied that for some kinds of poetry the *intrusion* of certain ulterior ends may, and often does, lower their value; but there seem plainly to be other kinds of poetry in which its value as poetry definitely and directly depends upon the ulterior ends involved. Consider the Psalms, Isaiah, the New Testament, Dante, the *Pilgrim's Progress*, Rabelais, any really universal satire, Swift, Voltaire, Byron.

"In all these cases the consideration of ulterior ends has been certainly essential to the act of composing. That needs no arguing; but, equally, this consideration of the ulterior ends involved is inevitable to the reader."[1]

Dr Richards cites *The Ancient Mariner* and *Hartleap Well* as cases where the consideration of ulterior ends by the reader does tend to lower poetic value, for the reason that ulterior ends do not really enter into either poem. He suggests that we may agree with Bradley, so far as he is merely enforcing his point in relation to such cases. "But", he continues, "he fails to notice—it is only fair to say that few critics seem ever to notice it—that poetry is of more than one kind, and that the different kinds are to be judged by different principles....Dr Bradley is misled by the usual delusion that there is in this respect only one kind of poetry, into saying far more than the facts of poetic experience will justify."[2]

[1] *P.L.C.* pp. 75–6. [2] *Ibid.* p. 77.

Now it seems to me that Dr Richards is much too ready to attribute blindness to Bradley. Let us note Bradley's exact words: they relate to the poet '*in the act* of composing' and the 'reader *in the act* of experiencing'. A great deal precedes the act of composing, and is essential to it, as a preliminary. The poet, like other people, is bound to consider moral values in his day to day life. He will form opinions, and perhaps argue about them; feel emotions, and perhaps translate them into action. Opinion and feeling may even combine into a passionate philosophy, with which he may, in season and out of season, plague his friends. But if he is to write a philosophic poem, the philosophy must have entered deeply into his imaginative life, and become an object of contemplation, before he sets himself to the final act of composing. If, while he is in the act of composing, contemplation fails him, and he addresses himself directly to the propagation of his views—an end ulterior to the imaginative experience of poetry—his work is almost certain to be taken out of its proper atmosphere, and to lose in poetic value.

It needs no arguing that in the case, say, of *The Pilgrim's Progress*, long consideration of moral values was essential, as a preliminary, to the act of composing. But the poetic value of the book is greatest in passages where the moral purpose, though always present, loses separate existence in the sharp and urgent vision: passages where Bunyan, in the act of composing, was too much concentrated on the object of imagination to consider the moral end ulterior to it. Conversely, the poetic value suffers where the moral purpose asserts its independence.

And so with all work where ulterior values are prominent and active. Such work belongs to the world of poetry, so far as it speaks to the contemplative imagination. It may, in particular cases, have a doubtful claim, or no claim at all, to citizenship of that world. Satire, for example, if it is merely personal and spiteful, belongs to the real world, unless there is a special limbo set aside for verse that is not poetry. In other cases, the work may have a clear title to double citizenship. It may be at home in the poetic world, and yet its moral or religious importance may be as great or greater. And, of course, the relative importance of the poetic and other values may change very much with time, as—to take an obvious example—in the case of Dante.

Truly, as Dr Richards would have us notice, poetry is of more than one kind: but the different kinds are to be judged on one plane, i.e. by the single test of imaginative experience. Compare the poetic worth of a psalm, for example *The Lord is my Shepherd*, with that of Herrick's *Whenas in silks my Julia goes*. We need not trouble about any ulterior values, in our delight with the latter poem. The psalm, on the other hand, obviously has such values. It springs from a soil into which a beatific mood of trustfulness and worship has sunk deep. Out of the soil, so impregnated, comes—as it could come from no other— the imaginative experience created through the original words of the psalm, and created anew through the words of the English translation. That experience would have been impossible but for consideration by the psalmist, before the act of composing, of the divine comfort and mercy: but its poetic worth is selfless, purely contemplative, and quite distinct from the happy dependence on divine comfort which the words may bring to the reader as an ulterior value. To compare the poetic worth of the psalm with that of Herrick's lines, we must exclude its ulterior value, as such. This is difficult: for the same reason it is difficult to compare the poetic worth of Vaughan's *They are all gone into the world of Light!* with that of Keats' *Ode to Autumn*. But the task of comparison would be still more difficult, if we had to compare the imaginative *plus* the ulterior moral and religious values of Vaughan's poem with the purely imaginative value of the Ode. The critic who follows Bradley will not have to face so vast an enterprise, with its valuation of all values.

Bradley is, of course, quite aware that there are different kinds of poetry, and that moral purpose has sunk deep into the soil from which some kinds spring. And so he writes that "Shakespeare's knowledge or his moral insight, Milton's greatness of soul, Shelley's 'hate of hate' and 'love of love', and that desire to help men or make them happier which may have influenced a poet in hours of meditation—all these have, as such, no poetical worth: they have that worth only when, passing through the unity of the poet's being, they reappear as qualities of imagination, and then are indeed mighty powers in the world of poetry."[1]

The case of the reader is parallel to that of the poet. Where, as in the examples cited by Dr Richards, ulterior values are involved, it may be agreed that their consideration is inevitable: but, once again, only as a preliminary. The reader must consider the ulterior values, in such a

[1] *O.L.P.* p. 7.

way as to understand them, and to accept them, if he can, for the sake of the experience which the poem offers. This consideration will have to take place during and between a number of imperfect acts of experiencing. The poetic value of those early, preliminary experiences will, in any case, be defective owing to the lack of a complete understanding, and the attempt to understand may still further lower it by distracting the reader from the poem's sensuous appeal.

It is possible that the attempt may never succeed. The very virtues of the reader may hinder him. The mature thinker may find himself repelled, as Mr Eliot confesses himself to be, by the adolescent thought of Shelley, and the result may be a failure to enter into his poetry. And the reader who has a nerve exquisitely sensitive to pain in the world may be driven, like Alice Meynell, to take the moral of *The Ancient Mariner* too seriously, as Dr Richards convicts her of doing;[1] and his enjoyment may continue to be troubled. These things are largely a matter of the mental and emotional make-up of the individual. Many obstacles to full appreciation may, however, be overcome by good will and the effort of sympathy. Moreover, consideration of the structure of a poem, that is to say, of the part played in it by various components, may cause the offending feature to sink into the background, and the perspective may thus be entirely altered. On this point Dr Richards gives useful and much-needed advice.

If the attempt at understanding is finally successful, it will have been abundantly worth while. For the reader will now be in a position to enjoy, without distraction,

[1] *P.L.C.* p. 76.

the full imaginative experience of the poem, ignoring for the time 'the beliefs, aims and particular conditions' which belong to him 'in the other world of reality'. He will be in a position to enter into the world of poetry and 'possess it fully'. This last will be the full act of experiencing, which the critic must endeavour to recapture in judging, as from within, the poem's poetic worth. It is quite wrong to suppose that Bradley gives any countenance to the sickly idea, rightly contemned by Dr Richards, that there is a pure aesthetic *approach* to profound poetry. What he says is concerned, not with the approach to poetic experience, but with the final destination, the self-rewarding act. The distinction is overlooked by Dr Richards in his attack on Bradley's third position, but it is of vital importance.

Bradley admits that the contemplative imagination, to which alone poetry speaks, is 'saturated with the results of "real" experience': [1] that is to say, in terms of another metaphor, he does not deny the abundance of traffic on the way of approach that connects life and poetry. But the connection may not ineptly be pictured as 'underground': for whatever passes through it into the poetic world suffers a deep change in passing. It is emancipated from the laws of the real world, to win the freedom of a world 'independent, complete, autonomous'.

[1] *O.L.P.* p. 7.

Chapter XIII

CREATION OF EXPERIENCE

Definition of a Poet

An artist is one who, through the imposition of form on his particular material, creates for himself, and potentially for others, a unified contemplative experience, highly objective in character: a poet is one who, through the metrical arrangement of words, creates an experience of this kind; and a metrical arrangement of words having such an effect is a poem.

What is meant by a 'unified contemplative experience' will, I hope, have been made clear in Chapter ix, while Chapter x explains what is meant by calling it 'highly objective in character'. When I say that the poet 'creates', I imply that his true work, like that of other artists, is to make, not to express or communicate. This part of the definition will now be considered.

As a minor matter, it will be observed that the writer of poetic or strongly rhythmical prose falls within the genus *artist*, but not within the species *poet*. Further, consistently with my practice throughout I give the name 'poem', not to the experience (although that is the end-all of poetry), but to the words through which the experience is created; this popular usage is much the most convenient, and on the whole makes for clarity.

Creation as distinct from Communication. The question we have to face is the kind of relationship which exists between the final experience given by a poem and the relevant earlier experience of the poet. There is always an essential difference. The value of the final experience

lies in an activity of the mind which is aroused through
the sound, etc., and the meaning of words (particular
words in a particular metrical arrangement), and which
is dependent upon those words, no less for the poet than
for his reader. This is *poetic* value. The earlier experience,
on the other hand, seeks a development in words which
as yet it lacks; it may have value, and even, in particular
cases, a value exceeding that of the final experience, but
it has not a strictly poetic value. And we shall see that
the poetic value cannot be simply the expression or
communication of the non-poetic.

A possible misunderstanding had better be cleared out
of the way at once. An emotion, a thought or a system
of thought *in an abstract sense,* that is to say, abstracted
from the context of the poet's experience (crystallized
out of its flow), can be expressed and communicated in
a poem, in the sense that it can also be *abstracted* from the
experience which the poem creates. In this sense the
work of some contemporary poets can be said to express
a belief in Communism. But poetry, although it may
possibly be a persuasive vehicle for such expression, is
in its essential nature concerned with something entirely
different, namely imaginative experience in all its con-
creteness. And so the question we have to consider is
whether the final experience, as a *concrete* whole, imparted through a poem, is the communication of an earlier
experience, again as a *concrete* whole.

To what earlier experience can we most hopefully
look? Not, I think, even in the case of a nature-poem, to
the original sensations, to the moment when the lark was
heard or the rainbow seen; for these moments, however

impressive at the time, have been plunged in the unconscious, and their images, after submitting to a sea-change,
have been drawn up by memory into a new context.
Rather, it would seem, we should look to that active state,
enriched by memory, which impels the poet to write, that
experience (if such can be found) which he takes and keeps
before him, as an artist his model. For here we might
hope to find, in concrete form, the central aim of the
poet.

But the poet's experience develops in different ways.
At one end of the scale is the rare, and perhaps only ideal,
case of the lyric born complete. Beginning and end
coincide, so that, if we want an earlier experience, we
must delve through the unconscious to earlier conscious
happenings. And, if our psycho-analysis could lay them
bare, we should find that the poem, far from communicating that material, had utterly transformed it.

Far more often, the moment of insight in which, it may
be, a hidden analogy is seized, and a sensation or image
suddenly charged with spiritual depth, is accompanied by
no more than a provisional groping after speech. The
impelling experience has a degree of complexity and
coherence, but it falls far short in these respects of a poem.
It is compact of possibilities, some of which will have to
be sacrificed. In the fulfilment of those which survive,
words may play a less or a more conspicuous part. Words,
fashioned by generations of men, have an incalculable
store of meanings, not fixed, but not so elastic that any
individual can wholly bend them to himself; and the words
that offer to serve a poet's need, stirring tremors in him
with meanings kindred to his own, but not yet his, suggest

new elements with which he may supplement his experience. As Mr Sturge Moore writes, "when an author will go only where he wants to, he says good-bye to all felicities of language, which depend on his obedience to the suggestions of words".[1] The new-come word, which is approved because (for reasons, perhaps, obscure to the poet himself) it feels right, introduces a slight, subtle but permeating change, and thus the poet may reach his goal after a score of deviations from the course that originally seemed to be marked out. As the poem gets itself written, the attention of the poet is increasingly transferred from the first impelling experience to the divergent experience which he is creating through the words. For this latter experience becomes more and more prophetic of its end, and, as it does so, its demands become more clear and more insistent, just as the last strokes of a painter's brush are dictated, not by the landscape as he first saw and felt it, but by all that he has come to feel in the form and colour on his canvas. Here again, then, the final experience is a new creation, not communicating anything that exists apart from itself.

The only case that gives rise to difficulty is found where the words of the poem are so unobtrusive that they seem to the reader to be transparencies, through which he sees the poet expressing what he feels apart from them. The simplicity of art is sometimes deceptive, but is it always so? Many people, contemplating in bereavement the memories private to themselves, have found the sum of their sorrow implied in the poignant feeling of difference. "But she is in her grave, and oh, The difference to me!"—did not Wordsworth experience that

[1] *Armour for Aphrodite*, p. 66.

same emotion, begotten by contemplation on grief, and merely communicate it, better than others, in words that exactly fitted it and added nothing?

It seems pedantic to say no, but what is pedantic for ordinary purposes may be sensible and necessary for exact argument. We may concede a good deal. In the first place, it may happen that, as the poet builds up his experience, words continue for a time to be no more than a light and temporary scaffolding. New images come in, depending little on verbal suggestion, or there is a sifting out of a mass of material, the contemplative eye divining deeper significance in the combination of a few selected aspects, where implication has a strength denied to full statement. Contemplation may thus proceed some way in a world the values of which have hardly begun to be poetic in the strict sense: and such a brooding over actual past experience, not yet modified by speech, must often have preceded the birth of Thomas Hardy's poems— a brooding of such intensity that place and time and mood take on the stillness, the composure, of art. Moreover, when the time for composition has come, the poet can do his best not to let words deflect him from his course, rejecting words which seem to contribute a tone of experience not in accord with his aim. To some extent he stubbornly goes 'only where he wants to', at the cost of sacrificing felicities of language.

But only to some extent. The poem, which must be judged as a whole, inevitably has a different effect from the ranging, poignant experience that has no fixed words to accompany it. All contemplation has, indeed, a tran-quillizing effect, but it does not achieve the same stability, unity or clarity as the 'unified contemplative experience' created through words. And each of these three qualities is important. Even in the sifting out of selected aspects, words have a way of being dictators. The poet may be single-minded in the effort to convey a particular experience as a whole, and yet the words, the self-effacing words that he finds most apt, reveal to him that only certain of its elements can be fused into the whole which he is creating. It is impossible to say why this is so: it is impossible to say exactly how the subtleties of sound (which exercise individual power even in the simplest language) condition this total unity. But *that* it does so happen is beyond all doubt.

If we say, then, that *some* poems are a 'communication' of the poet's experience, we must add a proviso that the correspondence is always imperfect. The term is apt to insinuate the false idea that a perfect poem would be the perfect expression of (i.e.' would perfectly correspond with) an unformulated experience existing independently in the poet's mind. There is, in fact, little excuse for speaking of communication in the sense we have been discussing, since there is another term applicable to all poems alike with equal accuracy and entire sufficiency, viz. the term 'creation'.

I say in my definition that the poet creates both for himself and potentially for others. The creation 'for himself' is alone sufficient to constitute him a poet: but, since words are common to all men, he creates for others as well, unless he suppresses what he writes or cannot find any readers. The poem, then, is a communication in the sense that it creates *an* experience for reader as well as for poet, but even here it does not make common one and the same experience. The experience will differ, sometimes surprisingly, even among people who are equally intelligent and sympathetic. At least, however, it is an experience of the same class, an experience created through, and controlled by, words: a *poetic* experience.

This view is sharply at variance with that of Dr Richards, and a comparison may be instructive. "The two pillars", he writes, "upon which a theory of criticism must rest are an account of value and an account of communication."[1] "Sometimes art is bad because communication is defective, the vehicle inoperative; sometimes because the experience communicated is worthless; sometimes for both reasons."[2]

Now, if it sometimes happens that the relevant experience of the artist has worth or value, but that there is a failure in communication, we may ask whether this implies—

(a) that the valuable relevant experience is to be found in the unformulated day to day experience of the artist's life, and that communication fails, because the work of art fails to express it; *or*

(b) that the valuable relevant experience is that created by the artist for himself through his completed work, and that communication fails merely because other people are so different from him.

If, as I have argued, what the artist does is to create, and primarily to create for himself, it is clear that (b) is right. But, if this is so, the account of value must include

[1] *P.L.C.* p. 25.   [2] *Ibid.* p. 199.

a discussion of the artist's method, style and technique, while the account of communication will be concerned solely with the question how much the artist and his public have in common, the question (as Dr Richards well puts it) of the 'normality' of the artist. In such a case the account of communication is a very secondary matter.

It is clear that Dr Richards, in spite of occasional remarks that seem inconsistent, holds that (*a*) is correct, and not (*b*). Thus he tells us that "it is as a communicator that it is most profitable to consider the artist".[1] A communicator, he means, of moral values which (in his sense of 'moral') are the only values: for "the world of poetry ...is made up of experiences of exactly the same kind as those that come to us in other ways".[2] He emphasizes the superior organization of values in the day to day experience of the artist. "In order to keep any steadiness and clarity in his attitudes the ordinary man is under the necessity on most occasions of suppressing the greater part of the impulses which the situation might arouse. He is incapable of organizing them; therefore they have to be left out. In the same situation the artist is able to admit far more without confusion."[3] Again, he writes of the artist that "to make the work 'embody', accord with, and represent the precise experience upon which its value depends is his major pre-occupation".[4] What is meant by the 'precise experience'? He quotes certain lines as an example of defective communication, "in which it is likely that the *original* experience had some value".[5] It

---

[1] *P.L.C.* p. 27.
[2] *Ibid.* p. 78.
[3] *Ibid.* p. 184.
[4] *Ibid.* p. 26.
[5] *Ibid.* p. 199—italics mine.

is thus evident that the value of which an account must be given by the theory of criticism is to be looked for, not in the final experience of the poem (except as communicating it), but in some earlier experience of its author.

The error here is fundamental. Dr Richards makes too wide a gap between the day to day experience of the poet and that of the ordinary man. He gives the impression that the poet is always in a state of greater receptivity, and that his ordinary life is a model of organization. I suggest, on the contrary, that the creative impulse, moving amid a wealth of matter no doubt partially organized, makes for disharmony that can only be resolved by the creative act. As Dr Richards says, "we all know people of unusually wide and varied possibilities who pay for their width in disorder, and we know others who pay for their order by narrowness".[1] Precisely. And I do not believe that poets and other artists are to be placed in a third class, doubly blessed with wide and ordered experience, the communication of which to others is their sacred task. They usually pay for their width in disorder, or rather in a partial order which is more disturbing than a total confusion. In their wide ranging they achieve subtle connections and interrelations denied to the ordinary mind. But these are such as to cause a ferment: they are incomplete, they nag at the memory and cry out for further development. "Anyone who has ever been visited by the Muse is thenceforth haunted."[2] And development can only be secured through contemplation, and with certainty and wholeness, only when it is pressed

[1] *P.L.C.* p. 288 (Appendix A).
[2] T. S. Eliot, *The Use of Poetry and The Use of Criticism*, p. 69.

through to the final act of creation, the unified contemplative experience of art, in which turmoil is replaced by balance and harmony. And every such experience is a *new* creation.

Dr Richards makes a very just discrimination between 'formative' and 'repetitive' imagination, writing that "the imaginative construction is always at least as much determined by what is going on in the present as by what went on in the past, *pasts* rather, whence it springs",[1] and that "the effect of any element depends upon the other elements present with it".[2] There are passages, too, in which he recognizes the vital and controlling importance of the formal elements. It should follow that, as I have maintained, the final experience imparted by the poem differs essentially from the past experience. Yet Dr Richards regards it as a communication of the past experience, and treats the formal elements, since they have the most 'uniform' effect on impulses, as potent for such communication rather than for the creation of something unique and new. There is a contradiction here. It is no use to point out that, while the poem is a fresh organization, the elements which it organizes include those of the original experience. For value, in Dr Richards' view, is purely quantitative, and the whole virtue of any experience lies in the number of different and perhaps conflicting impulse-groups it is able to reconcile. And this, of course, is a matter of organization, and the organization is admittedly new.

The truth is that, unless the new organization is effective, the poet fails to *create* an experience. The poem

[1] *P.L.C.* p. 192.   [2] *Ibid.* p. 179.

which Dr Richards quotes as an example of the defective communication of an 'original experience' which may have had some value is as follows:

THE POOL

Are you alive?
I touch you,
You quiver like a sea-fish.
I cover you with my net.
What are you—banded one?

"The reader here supplies too much of the poem", he comments. "Had the poet said only, 'I went and poked about for rocklings and caught the pool itself', the reader, who converts what is printed above into a poem, would still have been able to construct an experience of equal value; for what results is almost independent of the author."[1]

H. D., who wrote the lines, is a poet of slender but real distinction, normal enough to win appreciation, and she may have had an 'original' experience of some value. But if, in this unfortunate instance, she has not written a poem, if it is left to the reader to convert her lines (or their sense) into a poem, it is plain that she has failed to create an experience either for herself or for the reader. *The private non-poetic value of the poet's day to day experience has not been replaced by an experience of different, poetic value, created (as it can only be created) through words.* We have to discriminate carefully between these values, and it is 'most profitable' to consider the poet, not as a communicator, but as a creator. When he successfully creates for

[1] *P.L.C.* p. 200.

himself, he need not worry about communication. His poem will *ipso facto* be a communication, in the sense that it will offer to readers, whose minds are not too differently constituted from his, a new and valuable experience, in some degree similar to the new and valuable experience which it gives him. The experience will be *new*. The name 'poet' is, after all, right. He is a maker.

Chapter XIV

REALITY AND FACTS OF MIND

It is not to be supposed that the contemplative experience of poetry is an inactive state. All contemplation, whether poetic or otherwise, is tranquil, requiring for its exercise a retirement from the world of overt action. It enables us to endure, and to accept without flinching, what in that world is full of pain or terror: but if—to borrow the terms of St Augustine—the contemplative is *semper quietus*, he is also in some degree *semper agens*. That is to say, the tranquil state is also emotional. In particular, the creative emotion of the poet is not reached, as Wordsworth says, 'by a species of reaction' from tranquillity: it is rather a changing and heightening of emotion, with disturbance, but without loss, of tranquillity. The creative effort, reinforced by the stimulus of the words and rhythms in which the poet is labouring, may be very severe. But with it goes an awareness of the growing assembly of ideas and images, in their intricate relations and approach to coherent order: and this awareness has a tranquillizing as well as an exciting power.

The vital activity which seeks to fuse the whole assemblage into one is called by Coleridge the 'secondary Imagination'. He contrasts it with fancy in the following much-debated passage:

"The Imagination then I consider either as primary, or secondary. The primary Imagination I hold to be the living power and prime agent of all human perception, and as a repetition in the finite mind of the eternal act of creation in the infinite I AM. The secondary Imagination I consider as an echo of the former, co-existing with the conscious will, yet still as identical with the primary in the *kind* of its agency, and differing only in *degree*, and in the *mode* of its operation. It dissolves, diffuses, dissipates, in order to re-create: or where this process is rendered impossible, yet still at all events it struggles to idealize and to unify. It is essentially *vital*, even as all objects (*as* objects) are essentially fixed and dead.

"FANCY, on the contrary, has no other counters to play with, but fixities and definites. The fancy is indeed no other than a mode of memory emancipated from the order of time and space; while it is blended with, and modified by that empirical phenomenon of the will, which we express by the word Choice. But equally with the ordinary memory the Fancy must receive all its materials ready made from the law of association."[1]

The distinction between imagination and fancy is valid and useful, if they are interpreted, not as faculties of the mind, but as differing modes of activity between which the mind passes in its ever-changing organization. Observe the emphasis laid on the vital energy of the imaginative mode. It was Coleridge's outstanding virtue that he broke away from the traditions of English philosophy, of Locke and Hume and Hartley, to recognize the mind as a living and growing, self-creating process. The change in him was, no doubt, fundamentally due to personal experience, as he became increasingly aware of the pressure—the urgency and volume—of his own thinking and feeling. It was assisted, however, by early

[1] *Biographia Literaria*, Ch. 13.

study of Plotinus and other mystics. Then, with a mind already re-directed, he began to absorb German metaphysics, Schelling, in particular, appearing to offer a reasoned exposition of the new faith. Schelling's doctrine of the creative activity of mind did indeed chime in with the Neoplatonic view, but, in their ultimate issue, the two were not really consonant. With Schelling the Absolute could only realize itself through the activity of the individual subject, and supremely through the activity of the artist, while with Plotinus the Divine Intelligence was the perfect and transcendent source of Man, and Nature, and all Being. Coleridge was led by experience and predilection to favour the Neoplatonic view. The presence, in *Biographia Literaria*, of large tracts of Schelling side by side with quotations from Plotinus is significant. They never lost their separateness, though Coleridge persisted in the vain attempt to bring them into harmony.

Historically, Coleridge takes his place in the wide movement of thought leading, in the present day, to the philosophy of M. Bergson. M. Bergson, too, has his link with Schelling. For he was influenced by Ravaisson, who, as a young man in 1835, attended the lectures of Schelling at Munich. When properly understood, the work of the great French philosopher is hardly less remarkable for the severity of its intellectual discipline than for the clearness of its basic intuition of *la durée*. All through his writings he pursues the duality of spirit and matter: on the one side, growth, creation, freedom, the indivisible movement of time as it is lived (*la durée*); on the other side, petrefaction, repetition, automatism, the infinitely divisible both in space and, when once it has assumed the immobility of the past, in time: the former a sphere in which the analytical intellect must labour hard under the close surveillance of intuition, the latter a sphere in which it is at home and can be given free way. The general nature of this duality was deeply, if obscurely, felt by Coleridge; it was illustrated with strange vividness in his life.

There is an interesting parallel between Coleridge's account of imagination and fancy, and a passage in M. Bergson's *Les Deux Sources de la Morale et de la Religion*, which I will set down here. In reading of '*l'émotion originale et unique*', we may remember Coleridge's dictum, in a letter, that "deep thinking is attainable only by a man of deep feeling".

"Quiconque s'exerce à la composition littéraire a pu constater la différence entre l'intelligence laissée à elle-même et celle que consume de son feu l'émotion originale et unique, née d'une coincidence entre l'auteur et son sujet, c'est-à-dire d'une intuition. Dans le premier cas l'esprit travaille à froid, combinant entre elles des idées, depuis longtemps coulées en mots, que la société lui livre à l'état solide. Dans le second, il semble que les matériaux fournis par l'intelligence entrent préalablement en fusion et qu'ils se solidifient ensuite à nouveau en idées cette fois informées par l'esprit lui-même: si ces idées trouvent des mots pré-existants pour les exprimer, cela fait pour chacune l'effet d'une bonne fortune inespérée; et, à vrai dire, il a souvent fallu aider la chance, et forcer le sens du mot pour qu'il se modelât sur la pensée. L'effort est cette fois douloureux, et le résultat aléatoire. Mais c'est alors seulement que l'esprit se sent ou se croit créateur. Il ne part plus d'une multiplicité d'éléments tout faits pour aboutir à une unité composite où il y aura un nouvel arrangement de l'ancien. Il s'est transporté tout d'un coup à quelque chose qui paraît à la fois un et unique, qui cherchera ensuite à s'étaler tant bien que mal en concepts multiples et communs, donnés d'avance dans des mots."[1]

M. Bergson is writing of 'all work, however imperfect, which has any element of creativeness', the work of the philosopher enquiring into reality and, no less, the work of the poet. When the poet '*se croit créateur*', he is inclined, very often, to think he is unveiling the real. M. Bergson himself tells us, in one passage, that the aim of the arts, including poetry, is to bring us face to face with reality.[2] Utterances of this kind (often meaning quite different things) are common enough in English authors, and are sometimes very superficial. With Coleridge, however, it was a deep conviction that poetry and philosophy are somehow at one in the quest of 'bright Reality'. What, then, is the theory of poetry to say?

I suggest that the theory of poetry is only concerned to a limited extent. It may affirm this much, that poetry gives an experience of more than common vitality and value. But whether that experience implies a reality *beyond itself*, or whether it is one with a *wider* reality— these are general questions for metaphysics. It may well be that the poetic experience has deep meaning for the philosopher. But, whatever it does or does not imply, the experience for its own sake, and not for the sake of its

---

[1] *Les Deux Sources de la Morale et de la Religion*, p. 48.

[2] *Laughter* (tr. from the French by Cloudesley Brereton and Fred Rothwell), p. 157.

implications, is the true and proper aim of poetry. That a particular poem seems to open the mind to a reality beyond itself may be a valuable element in our experience of it. It is valuable as a 'fact of mind'. But how many incompatible realities should we have to face, if we were to translate all these facts into doctrines, and try to found a philosophy upon them!

In his book *Coleridge on Imagination* Dr Richards does well to insist on the facts of mind, and we may deprecate with him the easy inference from emotional harmony to intellectual truth. A poetic utterance is to be taken as representing a fact of mind, as being true to "the history of the speaker's mind, and his feelings and attitudes in the moment of speaking, and conditions of their governance in the future": when the utterance is so taken, then, "in the examination of its structure and functions we shall be at work on the theory of poetry".[1] With this we may connect the perfectly valid conception of the poet as a maker of myths, which are accepted for their own sake, and are not judged, like scientific statements, by their truth as doctrines. We accept them—to apply words of Coleridge—with "that negative faith, which simply permits the images presented to work by their own force, without either denial or affirmation of their real existence by the judgment".[2]

The poet's myth-making activity is the imagination, the 'synthetic and magical power' as Coleridge named it. '*Magical*' perhaps—just as the postulate of philosophy, KNOW THYSELF, may be 'heaven-descended'—but on that account the more to be scrutinized. Dr Richards

[1] *Coleridge on Imagination*, pp. 143–4.   [2] *B.L.* ch. 22.

propounds the view that "with more self-knowledge we could live in a world which was *both* a transcription of our practical needs for exact prediction and accommodation, *and* a mythology adequate to the whole of our spiritual life".[1] Everything, he would persuade us, is myth. In the old days, when it was thought that religion or philosophy or science could give us Reality, poetry, as mere myth, was relegated to second rank. But "if we grant that all is myth, poetry, as the myth-making which most brings 'the whole soul of man into activity' (*B.L.* ii. 12) and as working with words, 'parts and germinations of the plant' and, through them, in 'the medium by which spirits communicate with one another' (*B.L.* i. 168), becomes the necessary channel for the re-constitution of order."[2] Poetry must take the place of religion, supply the spiritual needs of man, and build up the new age!

This is a vastly arrogant claim. There would be no need to object to the world of science being described as a myth, if Dr Richards were consistent in saying that it is the 'changing picture' of the world formed by the scientist which is the myth. Similarly, there would be no need to take offence at religion being described as myth, if it were merely intended to say that religion, like poetry, may be regarded as an expression of the nature and needs of man, and in so far as mythical. But to go further, and assert that science and religion are myths *and nothing else*, implies a baseless world about which argument is useless. It would be outside my province, however, to discuss the loss of status which science and religion are supposed to have

[1] *C. on I.* p. 171.   [2] *Ibid.* p. 228.

suffered. Let me rather consider certain limitations to the power of the poetic myth.

The myths of poetry are not make-belief, but are the projection of very real needs and desires. And since these human needs are insistent as well as complex, the myths cannot easily suffer from the discoveries of science. This is clear: for the world of our experience is the coloured world of our senses and emotions, and our nature expresses itself in anthropomorphic ideas. It is a world very different in richness from the abstract, scientific world.

Yet the discoveries of science do percolate through the mind (though far less than we might suppose) so as to affect the sort of myth which it can create or accept. When a myth not only clashes, but clashes in a way that cannot be ignored, with scientific belief, it loses power and no longer satisfies a need. Or, again, consider philosophy. When poetry takes philosophic ideas into its texture, it must, *so far as it challenges thought*, be subject to the same kind of test as philosophic prose. Its intuition must have a certain clarity, its reasoning a certain coherence. We ought to examine closely any claim that poetry can reconcile, better than prose statement, intellectual doctrines which appear to conflict.

Such a claim is made by Dr Richards, who takes as an example Coleridge's use of the Aeolian harp, responding to diverse winds, as an image of the mind. It seems to me that in this test case—perhaps the climax of his study of Coleridge—his failure is complete. He suggests the following formulation of the two doctrines said to be reconciled through the Wind Harp image: it will be noted that the first leans rather to Neoplatonism, the second to the viewpoint of Schelling:

"1.	The mind of the poet at moments, penetrating 'the film of familiarity and selfish solicitude', gains an insight into reality, reads Nature as a symbol of something behind or within Nature not ordinarily perceived.

"2.	The mind of the poet creates a Nature into which his own feelings, his aspirations and apprehensions, are projected.

"In the first doctrine man, through Nature, is linked with something other than himself which he perceives through her. In the second, he makes of her, as with a mirror, a transformed image of his own being."[1]

Dr Richards contends that the early Coleridge had an intuition of a fact of mind which is the 'ground and origin'[2] of these two doctrines, the realist and projective: that the doctrines are true only when taken together as interpreting the single fact of mind, 'the immediate self-consciousness in the imaginative moment':[3] that the ambiguity in Coleridge's thought in his poem *Dejection* (and, apparently, the ambiguity elsewhere, both in Coleridge and Wordsworth, as between the two doctrines) is rather to be named completeness: that "this ambiguity (or rather, completeness) in Coleridge's thought here and his peculiar use of the Wind Harp image, give us a concrete example of that self-knowledge, which ... was for him, both 'speculatively and practically', the principle of all his thinking":[4] that the Wind Harp image

---

[1] *C. on I.* p. 145.	[2] *Ibid.* p. 147.
[3] *Ibid.* p. 162.	[4] *Ibid.* p. 152.

can achieve a 'coalescence of the two doctrines':[1] that we must not identify the abstracted idea with the idea in the completeness it has *in* the poem:[2] that "poetry is the completest mode of utterance":[3] that Coleridge "very soon left the theory of poetry to become metaphysician and moralist":[4] that he was led astray by the abstract doctrines: that the doctrines, as such abstractions, "induce further facts of mind—apprehensions of them as *theories* or *beliefs*—and these, as Coleridge's own history shows, can become gross obstacles to the return of 'the philosophic imagination, the sacred power of self-intuition'".[5]

The two main passages quoted from Coleridge are:

> *O the one Life within us and abroad,*
> *Which meets all motion and becomes its soul,*
> *A light in sound, a sound-like power in light,*
> *Rhythm in all thought, and joyance everywhere.*
>
> .   .   .   .
>
> *And what if all of animated nature*
> *Be but organic Harps diversely framed,*
> *That tremble into thought, as o'er them sweeps*
> *Plastic and vast, one intellectual breeze,*
> *At once the Soul of each, and God of all?*
>
> The Aeolian Harp (1795).

> *O Wordsworth! we receive but what we give*
> *And in our life alone does Nature live:*
> *Ours is her wedding-garment, ours her shroud!*
> *And would we ought behold, of higher worth,*

---

[1] *C. on I.* p. 163.   [2] *Ibid.* p. 225.
[3] *Ibid.* p. 163.   [4] *Ibid.* p. 144.
[5] *Ibid.* pp. 165–6.

Than that inanimate cold world allowed
To the poor loveless ever-anxious crowd,
  Ah! from the soul itself must issue forth
A light, a glory, a fair luminous cloud
  Enveloping the Earth—
And from the soul itself must there be sent
  A sweet and potent voice, of its own birth,
Of all sweet sounds the life and element!

Dejection (1802).

On the first passage Dr Richards makes the comment that "we can, by weighting *all motion, animated nature, organic* and *thought*, make this more an account of the birth of the known from the mind than a perception of a transcendent *living* Reality without".[1] On the second passage, "as before, we cannot say, if we take the poem as a whole, that it contains the one doctrine rather than the other. The colours of Nature are a suffusion from the light of the mind, but the light of the mind in its turn, the shaping spirit of Imagination, comes from the mind's response to Nature:

> *To thee do all things live from pole to pole,*
> *Their life the eddying of thy living soul.*"[2]

What are we to say? If this poetry (although the second passage, taken by itself, seems clearly enough to be projective) can be read either way by a shift of emphasis, we may reasonably infer not a *fusion* of the two doctrines, but a *confusion*. At best it would seem that the mind alternates between them, with an inkling that each is

[1] *C. on I.* p. 148.   [2] *Ibid.* p. 152.

incomplete. That is a very different thing from fusion. Any poet much occupied with the doctrines, and veering in allegiance from one to the other, might be expected to express himself as Coleridge did. There is no escape from this conclusion, unless it is possible to read the poems in such a way as, while allowing proper weight to their intellectual structure, to transcend the distinction between the realist and projective positions.

Dr Richards tries to do so, and professes to solve Coleridge's ambiguity by analysing the ambiguous use of the term Nature. There is a world as prosaically perceived, an 'inanimate cold world', and we call it Nature (Sense III in the analysis): there is, on one side of this prosaic world, a world indefinitely enriched by the projection upon it of our images and feelings, and we call it Nature (Sense II): there is, on the other side of it a world thinned out from it, though still a product of our perceptions, the world of Physics, and we call it Nature (Sense IV): there is, also, an independent world to which the mind responds, and we call it Nature (Sense I).[1]

After a long and quite acceptable analysis on these lines, we are abruptly told that "in terms of such a multiple definition the gap between the two doctrines— that the mind can see God in or through Nature, and that it can only see itself projected—becomes an artificial product of a shifting of the senses of *Nature, mind*, and *see*. A fuller description of the 'facts of mind' from which the poet and the philosopher alike set out carries both doctrines as accordant functions, as uncontradictory interpretations."[2] A fuller description is indeed necessary,

[1] *C. on I.* pp. 157–61.   [2] *Ibid.* p. 162.

for the conclusion appears to be a complete *non sequitur*. Careful attention to the different meanings of 'Nature' gets us nowhere, and the long analysis is like the skilful patter of a conjuror which may conceal from the audience that he has never performed his trick.

Unfortunately, on second thoughts, Dr Richards shies away from a fuller description: "for any description in prose is itself a doctrine hard to keep from being just one or other of the two we are considering".[1] But, where prose fails, he would persuade us that poetry, as in the Wind Harp image, can succeed: he therefore refers us to the originative fact of mind itself for a coalescence of the two doctrines. I do not find any sign of such a coalescence in the poetry of Coleridge.

Further, I ask this question. In what sense can we look for the 'ground and origin' of the two doctrines in a single fact of mind? How is it even possible that they should coalesce?

A comparison may help. M. Bergson's doctrine of *freedom* has its ground and origin in a fact of mind, 'our own personality in its flowing through time—our self which endures'.[2] That fact, seized by intuition, implies freedom, as growth or creativeness. But if we reflect upon our activity when it is past—when it has ceased to flow—and if we then follow the analytical method ingrained in the intellect, we inevitably distort the original fact; we picture freedom not as the single thrust of life in the living, but as the choice between ready-made alter-

[1] *C. on I.* p. 162.
[2] *Introduction to Metaphysics* (tr. from the French by T. E. Hulme), p. 8.

natives. We spatialize time, introducing the deceptive image of a road with turnings to right and left: and, in so doing, we play into the hands of the determinist, who is never so happy as when mapping out the dead past. The opposing doctrines of free will (as ordinarily understood) and of determinism have nothing to do with the movement of life. They are intellectual constructions, which cannot be reconciled; their conflict, however, may lead us to examine more closely the activity which they profess to describe. This is what M. Bergson has done to such effect: and, having laid firm hold of his intuition, his 'immediate self-consciousness', he has been able to show how the false problem of free will arises. He has not reconciled the opposing doctrines, but has replaced them. His doctrine of freedom has its ground and origin in a fact of mind, in the full sense that it is *implicit* in the mind's energy, in its self-creating activity. On the other hand, the old opposing doctrines of free will and of determinism are implicit only in certain highly sophisticated facts of mind, induced by a train of intellectual analysis the greater part of which is common to both. Their ground and origin cannot, with any truth, be placed prior to that sophistication.

Now the realist and projective doctrines are, in like manner, intellectual constructions. The history of Man's emotions in the presence of Nature is exceedingly complicated. They have varied from age to age, both as to intensity, and as to the kind of explanation that has been found for them. The particular kind of explanation inevitably reacts on the emotional experience, very often deepening it, always giving it form and quality. The type of explanation according to which the heavens declare the glory of God, or of one God among many, is an early development: that according to which the light and glory are emanations or reflections of Man himself ("from the soul itself must issue forth") is a comparatively late product, and goes against the grain with simple people.

The strong and sometimes ecstatic emotion of Coleridge clamoured for an explanation with which it could come to terms. And, with the help of mystics and philosophers, it found these two, the realist doctrine and the projective, both—as Dr Richards rightly observes— 'of a lofty and exciting order'. The emotional experience, closing with either of these intellectual doctrines, embraces a new excitement: at the same time it gains in definition, and takes on a particular quality. The resulting state of mind is sophisticated, in so far as it is induced by a theory or belief presupposing the analytical activity of the intellect. Coleridge grasped at both doctrines, and both are reflected in his Nature poetry. That poetry is not to be taken as the outcome of a pure emotion in its undefined intensity, but is to be taken as true to "the history of the speaker's mind, and his feelings and attitudes in the moment of speaking, and conditions of their governance in the future".[1] The 'ground and origin' of the two doctrines is not to be found in anything more simple, anything less bound up with abstract conceptions.

How, indeed, could it be otherwise? For the doctrines have to do, not (like those relating to free will) with the nature of our activity in itself, but with the conception of a Person or power or thing in some manner outside us,

[1] *C. on I.* p. 143.

to whom or to which our activity relates. *We shall look in vain, then, for a reconciliation of the conflict, to our simple consciousness of living. The doctrines are born of abstract thought, and, if they are to be reconciled at all, it can only be through further conceptual thinking. And if the thinking were successful, as it never was with Coleridge, it would lead to a single new doctrine, bearing likenesses to each of the conflicting doctrines, acceptable to the imagination, and capable of being stated in prose.*

In many poems, of course, the prose meaning is tenuous, elusive, unimportant. Here we do not look for logical consistency; indeed a mad inconsequence of thought, or a queer mingling of logic and absurdity, may be an excellent basis for a poem of nightmare emotion. But the more intellectual the structure of the poem, the more do we require that the thought should be coherent, or at least that there should be 'some one predominant thought'. Such passages from Coleridge as those quoted above are highly intellectual, challenging the reader to think. And the reader, so challenged, cannot ignore the presence in them of two unreconciled views of Nature. The experience of the passages has value; for each doctrine is accompanied by its own exciting images and emotions and, where the doctrines conflict, those attendant upon one are at least partially fused with those attendant upon the other. But that is not the same thing as a fusion of the doctrines themselves, or of the whole content of the mind. The conflict of doctrines is sufficient in some degree to baffle the imagination in its struggle 'to idealize and to unify'. There is, in this degree, a definite shortcoming in the poetry.

I am not suggesting that a doctrine in a philosophical poem need be without logical flaw, or that it need be demonstrably true. It suffices that it should be coherent enough or, if you like, plausible enough, to be acceptable to the mind of the poet, the maker of myths: if, as a reasonable being, he can accept it, then, whether or no it corresponds to any reality outside his own mind, it may satisfy in him and in his reader wider needs than those of the intellect. There are many variants of the realist and projective doctrines which, taken severally, are quite acceptable to the imagination. And there are doctrines, also acceptable, which go some distance towards reconciling the two. An example may be found in Francis Thompson's essay, *Nature's Immortality*, and it is significant that, in a footnote to his rhapsodical prose, he writes as follows: "Be it observed that I am not trying to *explain* anything, metaphysically or otherwise, and consequently my language is not to be taken metaphysically. I am merely endeavouring analogically to *suggest* an idea. And the whole thing is put forward as a fantasy, which the writer likes to think may be a dim shadowing of truth." Coleridge was not so easily satisfied. The metaphysician in him was clamorous, and he was not content with a doctrine of Nature that should be acceptable to the imagination, but was seeking one that should also be convincingly true to the reason. He was, in fact, philosophizing in verse, and he compels us to approach the poems through his philosophy, just as if it were stated in prose. And we find no reconciliation: we find no single and consistent fact of mind, except when one doctrine holds the field for a time to the exclusion of the other.

According to Dr Richards, Coleridge's Wind Harp image was an example of his intuitive self-knowledge: Coleridge was led astray from the wholeness of his intuition by the two abstract doctrines, and these induced in him further facts of mind which hindered the return of the philosophic imagination. "Coleridge, as 'the years matured the silent strife', became more and more held by attitudes consonant with the Realist doctrine, less and less able to recover his earlier integral vision of the poet's mind."[1] Nothing could be more misleading. The Wind Harp image betrays the uncertainty of Coleridge's mind, already in 1795 confronted more or less clearly with the two exciting abstract doctrines which continued to fascinate him through life. Neither did he start with an intuition embracing the two doctrines, nor did he fulfil his ambition of fusing the doctrines into one.

We are told that Coleridge "succeeded in bringing his suggestions to a point from which, with a little care and pertinacity, they can be taken on to become a new science".[2] The science will enquire into the modes of poetic mythology which, it is claimed, have the power to satisfy all man's spiritual needs. Those who regard this claim as blasphemous or heretical are to be referred to the self-realizing intuition—"no answer will meet them unless it can induce a return to the 'self-realizing intuition' from which any answer must come. And argument is not the mode of inducing this."[3] If we are to judge from the one example pressed upon us by Dr Richards—his interpretation of Coleridge's attitude to Nature—the new

[1] *C. on I.* p. 166.　　　　[2] *Ibid.* p. 43.
[3] *Ibid.* p. 171.

science is to be founded on a misreading of the mind. How can we believe in the intuition of a fact of mind able to unify two doctrines which come from the intellect, and which the intellect cannot reconcile; a fact of mind, so grounded in the intellect, which cannot be described in prose and can only find expression in the 'ambiguity or rather completeness' of poetic utterance; a fact of mind, the possibility of which is supported by a solemn 'linguistic analysis' which explains nothing? We are in the region of abracadabra and pseudo-mysticism. By such means is it sought to enthrone the poet as the purveyor of all our spiritual needs, the creator of a new order in the world!

Chapter XV

POETIC EMOTIONS

It is not easy to form a sane view of the poet's influence on society. If we repudiate the extravagant claims of Dr Richards, we must beware of falling into the opposite error, as Mr Belgion has done in his papers *What is Criticism?* and *The Irresponsible Propagandist*.[1]

Man's highest aim, according to Dr Richards, is to order his impulses, so that as many as possible may have full and free satisfaction. And poetry may help towards this harmony of spirit—or, we should rather say, this poise of the nervous system—as nothing else can. It is 'the unique linguistic instrument by which our minds have ordered their thoughts, emotions, desires...in the past'.[2] On the contrary, asserts Mr Belgion, "we cannot utilize poetry for the ordering of our minds": and the reason for this inability (which 'disposes of' Dr Richards) is that we cannot learn from a poem itself that the emotions it 'imitates' are serious, or, again, that the emotions it arouses in the reader are serious: we must know in advance, from our experience of living, what emotions are serious and what are trivial. We must learn, not from poetry, but from life.[3]

Can this be a true or just account? Can it be right to make poetry so dependent, so derivative? Let us consider Mr Belgion's view in its context.

[1] *The Human Parrot*, pp. 97–116 and 74–96 respectively.
[2] *Practical Criticism*, p. 320.
[3] *The H. P.* pp. 111–12.

The poet, we are told, imitates emotions with which he need not himself be familiar, and seeks to produce related emotions in his readers. The emotions of life which he imitates may be more serious or less serious, and the imitation may be more skilful or less skilful. The *sine qua non* for the poet "is not emotional experience but knowledge of what words and what orders of words will produce emotion, and also the gift, and mastery of the gift, of setting such words out in rhythmic sequences".[1] The poet's own emotion is far from being the emotion which he seeks to produce in his readers; it is referable to the impulse to create, and to the process of creation, and it is, in particular, the enjoyment of skill.

The emotion which he seeks to produce in his readers is passive, spontaneous, naïve:[2] "we must believe that every work of art has been fashioned to produce but one effect in all who behold it, and if the technique, and the seriousness of the emotion, of a poem are going to be appreciated, one must first undergo that effect of the poem."[3] Most people stop short at the naïve experience of a poem. But the few who possess 'a double knowledge and a double sense of values', relating both to poetry and to life, detach themselves from the effect of the poem:[4] they view the effect from the outside, and pass beyond the naïve experience to that appreciation or criticism in which 'the fullest enjoyment'[5] of poetry lies. And this is "the appreciation or criticism of the poet's making and of the skill that has gone into that making. The poet, in Aris-

[1] *The H. P.* p. 112.   [2] *Ibid.* p. 76.
[3] *Ibid.* p. 78.   [4] *Ibid.* p. 114.
[5] *Ibid.* p. 116.

totle's language, 'imitates' emotion. The critic has first to see what means the poet has employed in his imitation of emotion, and how far the poet's employment of the means indicates mastery over them. Also the critic has to pass judgment on the emotion produced. His second duty is to see to what extent the emotion imitated is profound and serious.

"The specifically aesthetic emotion is delight in the contemplation of technical ability, as manifested in its result. The poet has made a thing, and the aesthetic emotion is the delight that accompanies contemplating this made thing in its well-madeness."[1]

Precise and symmetrical enough! But the scheme is surely a fine example of the deceitfulness of intellect. The poet, however he may vibrate to the suggestion of individual word or phrase, does not *know* what words and rhythmic sequences will produce emotion. He can only *find out* in the process of composition. For all creative activity is unforeseeable:

> *The poet is not lord*
> *Of the next syllable may come*
> *With the returning pendulum;*
> *And what he plans to-day in song,*
> *To-morrow sings it in another tongue.*[2]

And, if he is a sincere artist, he does not so much find out what *will* produce emotion in his readers, as find out what *does* produce emotion in himself. What the poet needs above all is creative energy, and a critical sense of words.

[1] *The H. P.* pp. 112–13.
[2] Francis Thompson, *Sister Songs.*

Words come to him in his creative mood, seeking to be
chosen, and he quickly apprehends the way in which this
word or that answers to his state of mind at the moment.
'State of mind', however, is a bad term; for his mind is
moving all the time, and an experience created through
words is all the time growing in him. He is his own reader,
and the experience which he creates for himself, as reader,
is essentially the aesthetic emotion, the emotion to which
the whole of his art is directed. During the process of
creation, he is in a turmoil. On the one hand, there are
the active emotions of the creator and the craftsman—the
impulse to make, and the enjoyment of skill in the performance of a difficult task. On the other hand, there is
the contemplative emotion which is developing through
the words of the poem, an emotion attended by premoni-
tions, but certainly not by foreknowledge, of the end. It
is the sign of achieved creation when the poet's contemplative experience (something new and unique, to which
it is dangerous to apply the word 'imitation') is complete
in itself and supersedes all others.

This final experience of the poet has been attained only
through a keen appreciation of the words and cadences
chosen: the perception of word-values is inherent in it.
And it is this experience, this emotion, which the poet
desires his reader to share in all its complexity. And the
reader may, to some extent, share it. Mr Belgion is
wrong, then, when he says that the emotion of the poet,
while composing a poem, "cannot be in the least the
emotion which he succeeds in producing later in the
reader".[1] The emotion which grows in him during

[1] *The H. P.* p. 112.

composition is increasingly akin to the emotion he will produce in the reader: and his final experience is closely akin, not to that of the naïve reader but to that of the reader "with a knowledge and sense of values of poetry and its technique".[1] As Mr Belgion says, the successful reader must appreciate or criticize the poet's skill. This is true, but it is not true that he begins by enjoying the poem in the same 'spontaneous or naïve way' as other people—the majority—who can get no further; nor is it true that he reaches his final goal in criticism or appreciation. "It is exciting", notes Mr Belgion, "to read about, and picture as we read, the barge Cleopatra sat in, a barge which

> *like a burnished throne*
> *Burned on the water.*

There is a higher and purer excitement in becoming aware of the extraordinary effectiveness in this passage of the word 'burned'."[2] For myself, I find it impossible to imagine the sensitive reader having to 'detach himself' from the effect of the words quoted, and to bring a critical battery to bear upon them from the outside, before becoming aware of the effectiveness of the word 'burned'. All that the reader can require is a moment's fugitive reflection, such as occurs intermittently in all aesthetic experience. The effectiveness is already implicit in the first contact with the words: the realization of it increases, not through a continued detachment in the reader, but through alternation between the critical attitude and the contemplative.

The criticism, then, which follows upon a supposedly

---

[1] *The H. P.* p. 115.   [2] *Ibid.* p. 77.

naïve initial experience is not the 'fullest enjoyment' of poetry. Criticism is not an end, but a means. This is equally true, both as to the pictorial or sensory quality of the experience, and as to its emotional quality. The critical attitude, with its own connoisseur delight, should always be auxiliary, helping towards a richer experience, one more like that of the poet and more like that which the poet wishes to produce. *It is the finally enriched experience—not any creative prelude for the poet, nor any critical interlude for the reader—which is the fullest enjoyment of poetry. Indeed, it is impossible to tell from anything except the final experience which the poem produces to what extent its emotion is serious, or its technique good.*

So, after all, we must learn from the poem itself, and Mr Belgion is mistaken in thinking we cannot do so. His argument, like several others considered in this book, depends on the introduction of clear-cut distinctions— treated as ultimate—into the flow of experience. We find this corner of his interesting intellectual world oddly static: he fails to understand the continuity of development in the experience of poet and reader alike.

Chapter XVI

THE POET AND SOCIETY

The final, and properly *poetic*, experience of poetry is contemplative; and this experience has undoubted value for the ordering of the mind. It is here that the influence of poetry, as poetry, lies. But we must glance for a moment at those other, incidental, effects in the realm of thought and conduct to which I alluded in my first chapter. For, as I said there, we may, both in preparation for the enjoyment of a poem and in after reflection upon it, be occupied with issues that are not contemplative, but moral or intellectual.

These effects are only secondary in the case of poems which give us a true contemplative experience. But they may be of real importance. For every kind of thought and passion enters into the world of poetic contemplation, and may, by analysis and reflection, be brought back into the workaday world, to influence our attitudes and behaviour. The poet cannot disclaim responsibility for the practical teaching that may be extracted from his work, although he is responsible as thinker or moralist, rather than as poet: for, as poet, he is the creator of experience which belongs to the contemplative world, not the practical.

But the art of poetry is very often not pure; it has some tincture of the practical or speculative about it. Many poems, indeed, fail to give us anything like a full contemplative experience. They distract us by their appeal to practical sentiment, or their sensuality, or their

moralizing, or their political propaganda. Or, again, the
failure may lie, not with the poet, but with ourselves.
Very much depends on the reader, as may be seen still
more clearly in the case of fiction—an art less pure than
that of poetry, and with incidental effects on society which
are, as a rule, much more pronounced. Many immature
readers, and readers without artistic sensibility, and
readers anxious to find excuse for freedom in sex relations,
must have failed to appreciate the genius and the seriousness of D. H. Lawrence, and have read him to their own
harm. This is the sort of consideration which makes the
problem of censorship so difficult. It is more than a little
ludicrous that Mr T. S. Eliot, in his *Thoughts after
Lambeth*, should have taken the fifty bishops to task for
having "missed an opportunity of disassociating themselves from the condemnation of these two extremely
serious and improving writers", Mr James Joyce and
D. H. Lawrence. Granted that the two are sometimes
'improving', and even extremely so, to a small minority,
they are obviously a real or potential danger to many. It
is to be hoped that the bishops, even if they had the finest
and most highly trained literary sense, would pause to
consider the weaker brethren!

The effects of which I am speaking, whether good or
bad, are, so to say, by-products of art, for they have
nothing to do with contemplation. They are comparable,
in this respect, with the influence of crude works, e.g.
a great many cinema shows, which do not pretend to any
poetic or artistic element. Such works belong to the
practical world, and when their moral tendency is bad,
their antithesis is not so much in art as in other practical

works whose tendency is good. For art belongs to a different order of experience, the contemplative.

Let us return, then, to that order. I have spoken of the special stability, unity and clarity of the contemplative experience created through poetry. But we may, of course, have contemplative experience apart from poetry or the other arts. A tumultuous emotion of joy or grief which affects us personally, or with which we actively sympathize, passes into a contemplative emotion which, if it 'imitates', also transforms it. The original emotion affects us in the world of action: if it does not always hurry us on to act overtly, yet it is a state of unrest and is attended by agitation of the nervous system. The emotion is increased in violence by the accelerated heartbeat or the lump in the throat. But it is not on that account fully or clearly realized: rather does consciousness become clearer as the call for action disappears, or the physical disturbance subsides. It is then that we possess ourselves in the known quality of our joy or sorrow.

Such contemplative experience is necessary for the full life. It is also the link between the world of action and the world of art. The emotion which at first dumbfounded us, or else deprived us of all reticence, has, in becoming clearer, become amenable to form. We may, indeed, say that anything which can be experienced in contemplative fashion is a proper subject for art. And anything that is not so experienced, is not yet a proper subject. What is, for example, physically disgusting cannot, *in isolation*, be contemplated; and, until it enters into a whole which is not disgusting and therefore can be contemplated, it is unfit for art. What we feel to be threatening to our lives or careers cannot be contemplated, until the threat is in some manner removed to a distance—usually through our seeing it in a longer, less personal perspective—and till then it is unfit for art. No narrower statement, such as that by Mr W. B. Yeats that "passive suffering is not a theme for poetry",[1] deserves to have a hearing.

Poetry has value, both directly and indirectly, for the ordering of the mind: directly, since the poetic experience is itself marked by fine order; indirectly, since it promotes a contemplative habit of mind. And contemplation is necessary not only for the artist, but, in some kind, for every man. The administrator, the statesman, men in great place, have need of it, if they would be better than narrowly efficient, unimaginatively able. To forfeit the leisure needed for it is a sore loss. "Nay, retire men cannot when they would, neither will they when it were reason; but are impatient of privateness even in age and sickness, which require the shadow; like old townsmen, that will be still sitting at their street-door, though thereby they offer age to scorn.... Certainly men in great fortunes are strangers to themselves, and while they are in the puzzle of business they have no time to tend their health either of body or mind. '*Illi mors gravis incubat, qui notus nimis omnibus, ignotus moritur sibi.*'"[2]

Contemplation, be it remarked, runs a different course for the man of action and for the artist. The man of action, winning his needed detachment, is, so to speak, once removed from the press of business, to which he may soon return with clearer sight and truer mastery. The artist is

[1] Introduction to *The Oxford Book of Modern Verse*, p. xxxiv.
[2] Bacon, *Of Great Place*.

twice removed—not in the Platonic sense that implies a
diminution of reality, but in the sense of a reality twice
changed, deeply enriched. I have said that contemplation
transforms the tumultuous emotion of joy or grief, and
makes it amenable to form. In ordinary life we find a few
words, or perhaps an image of sight or sound—a face or
a voice—in which to focus our experience; but these are
in the nature of signs, helping us to realize our contemplative emotion, to rest in it with as little essential change
as possible. If we are further impelled to the writing of
a poem, we may think that we are merely finding words
for an experience that remains unaltered. But this is the
common delusion about self-expression; if we are in fact
doing what we think, we are being most imperfect poets,
for we are not creating anything with a life of its own.
Instead, our poem needs to be set against, and sink into,
the background of our private and special experience, and
is indeed unworthy to be called a poem, even for ourselves
who understand it. It is rather a secret sign, pointing back
to the contemplative experience, personal and not created
through words, from which we set out. We are still but
once removed from the tumult of active life.

In the creation of a true poem, on the other hand, our
contemplative experience undergoes a vital change, until
something new is born, as a child winning separate life
from its mother. In this process, the magical power of
words calls into being a new and compelling experience
that is not dependent on the co-operation of a narrow or
particular mind-history. Thus is the experience twice
removed from the world of action, having a stability,
unity and clarity characteristic of art.

Tragedy, by common consent, has a pre-eminence in the twice-removed poetic world. It derives this, in part, from the eminence which it holds in the once-removed contemplative experience of life. Even at the single remove, we attain to a deep satisfaction of spirit in being able to contemplate what, on its first impact, stunned or overwhelmed us. Our emotions become ordered, taking their place in a world which opens out again with long vistas and many aspects. And so they can be reconciled with opposite emotions, and can, for those who have the transforming energy and the sense of words, be inter-fused with a thousand new suggestions. This *may* happen: but it requires a rare degree of detachment, and most tragic poems are based on sympathy with imagined woes, that find no actual place in the poet's memory of his own life.

Tragic poetry has a healing power which critics have even over-emphasized. It undoubtedly helps to do away with repressions, to reconcile impulses and resolve con-flicts. And through these agencies it liberates and en-larges the mind. But there is a danger nowadays of driving the curative theory too far, as Mr Michael Roberts does, when he writes that "the psycho-analyst cannot explain the actuality of good imaginative poetry, for the imaginative poet is concerned with those resolutions [of conflicts] which cannot yet be accomplished scientific-ally".[1] Mr Roberts does at least recognize, a few pages later, that "the human mind is not solely concerned with the avoidance of internal conflict":[2] but, under the in-fluence of Dr Richards, he is too much occupied with it

[1] *Critique of Poetry*, p. 103.   [2] *Ibid.* p. 106.

himself, so that he undervalues poetry which is 'content to call up a pleasant emotion by reference to interests which are already quite harmonious'.[1] Pleasant emotion indeed—at what a low ebb do critics seem to live! Let us rather hear of poems which are pervaded by a fantastic energy or a deep power of joy, creating an experience quiet with contemplation, not tragic but pulsingly, exuberantly alive!

The enjoyment of poetry, then, in all its wide range, takes a unique place in the world of contemplative experience. But it is a part of that world, not the whole, and it is a vital part only for readers who have special sensibility for word and metre and rhythm. For them poetry is an important part of experience; if life helps them to realize what is profound and serious in poetry, poetry in turn helps them to realize what is profound and serious in life.

But what of those who find satisfaction, not in poetry or its closest of kin, imaginative prose, but in music or painting or sculpture? If aesthetic experience is to take the place of religion, as some propose, why narrow it to poetry alone? Poetic experience may be more searching and comprehensive than that given by any of the other arts, but that is no excuse for shutting them out. Let us therefore, if we are going to proclaim a substitute for religion, proclaim it in Art, rather than one art alone. Even so, the proclamation will be vain, for contemplative experience, though extended to art in general, is too narrow. Better seek a substitute in the contemplative attitude to the whole of life, submitting ourselves to such

[1] *C. of P.* p. 105.

a training as that of which Miss Joanna Field tells in *A Life of One's Own.* "The automatic widening of mental focus which seemed to follow muscular relaxing brought a twofold deepening of experience, a flooding in of overtones both from present bodily awareness and from the past in wave after wave of memories. It was not that I turned away from the present in order to think of the past but that the past gave added richness to the present.... Experiencing the present with the whole of my body instead of with the pin-point of my intellect led to all sorts of new knowledge and new contentment. I began to guess what it might mean to live from the heart instead of the head."[1] The attitude or way of perceiving described has, despite the emphasis on its physical basis, a special affinity to religious contemplation, since its first principle is 'to attend to something and yet want nothing from it', and this principle applied to personal relationships gives a power of entering by sympathy into the lives of others. I doubt whether the discipline involved can be successfully attempted by many, and, admirable as it is, I do not suggest that it can, in its highest exercise, be all-sufficing: but at least to some natures of fine endowment it may offer both happiness and a foundation for the good life.

Poetry, on the other hand, is not, in essence, concerned with moral action. Its world is a twice-removed world, independent, autonomous, where contemplative experience is not a means, but an end in itself. The poet, I have said before, can achieve in his creative work a satisfying harmony both for himself and, in different degrees, for those who appreciate him. But it is a confusion of thought

[1] *A Life of One's Own*, p. 188.

to locate the highest moral value in such a harmony, however many and diverse impulses it may reconcile. The man who can attain it, in the degree that a poet or artist can, is the less likely to be impelled to seek balance and satisfaction elsewhere, in the active pursuance of a moral or religious ideal. Since he can find rest in his poetic contemplation, weariness will not 'toss him'[1] to the breast of God. From this standpoint the man who is absorbed in poetry may have more excuse than others for selfishness and moral neutrality. "The poem", as Mr Roberts well says, "which succeeds in producing an absolute internal harmony deprives the reader of all desire for action. The perfect artist finds beauty in good and evil alike, and has no motive for action, but is content to contemplate his God, the miracle which is the world"—a God (to quote from the preceding passage) 'dangerously remote and utterly non-moral'.[2]

But nevertheless, it may be said, a *God*, and therefore religion: and not only so, but a religion giving contentment. Yes, in the sense that any object of man's devotion —Caesar or Mammon, no less than Art—may metaphorically be called a God. And contentment certainly: but this is a small part indeed of any religious attitude worth the name. If religion were no more than a kind of dope, if it were a myth having for sole aim the avoidance of conflict, poetry might, for people of the right sensibility, replace it to positive advantage. But Christianity, in which the flesh is acknowledged to war against the spirit, and the spirit against the flesh, is a very different

---

[1] George Herbert, *The Pulley*.
[2] *C. of P.* pp. 208–9.

kind of religion. In it faith is intimately connected with
works. The religious contemplation of the Christian is
not, like poetic contemplation, a complete end in itself.
For it is the vision, however dim, of a Person whose
holiness forces upon the worshipper a sense of his own
deficiency and sin: of One who is the supreme example of
love in action: of One who offers grace and strength, but
no certain release from conflict. Thus, through more than
one channel, contemplation tends to action and, though
it have both joy and serenity, leads to the cry, never quite
silenced—Lord, what shall I *do* to be saved?

The final contemplative experience of poetry offers no
such incentive. It may even, in an unhappy age, hold up
the mirror to our disillusion, our sordidness, our unrest,
only at last to reconcile us to things as they are. It can
make boredom itself worth looking at, so that we become
interesting invalids in our own eyes. The mere recognition of our disease brings relief and, perhaps, keeps us
away from the doctor. "*The Waste Land* for many
readers"—so writes Mr Roberts—"fulfils the functions
of myth: because that poem was possible, life is valuable."[1]
This is too much. Mr Eliot's remarkable and historically
important poem has, I suspect, caused reactions of the
widest variety. So far as its readers, or a few of them, have
arrived at the internal harmony of contemplation, they
may have lost desire for action. But it seems to me that
the poem, as is the way with more explicit satire, carries
its own corrective. For its secondary effects are strong.
The appreciation of it calls for much preparation, much
after reflection, much intellectual activity of a kind to set

[1] *C. of P.* p. 208.

up discord. It is not only (nor, I think, wholly) a poem, but is also a moral panorama, and in its character as the latter, not as poetry, it has a direct concern with conduct. And, even so, it has the concern of the moralist who can at best prepare the way for religion, but can by no means usurp its place.

At the beginning of Chapter ix I briefly summarized the first eight chapters. It may be convenient if I now summarize the remainder.

We found that the attitude which leads to aesthetic experience is one of active but disinterested attention to the object of experience, whether it be a sense-object or, e.g., an idea or an action. When well developed, the attitude is one of contemplation, which is distinct from judgment or criticism, though these are latent in it and, in actual experience, frequently intervene. The attitude allows imagery, thought and emotion, however practically useless, to flow in freely, changing and enriching the object. While aesthetic experience occurs among very primitive people, it may be surmised that consciousness had first to free itself from close bondage to the needs of action (Chapter ix). Aesthetic experience is more objective than practical or speculative experience, in the sense that the self is more steadily absorbed in its object, that object being nothing but the present riches of consciousness. This objective aspect of aesthetic experience is more important for aesthetic theory than the illusion, so much stressed by Dr Santayana, under which we persist in regarding beauty as 'a quality of things'. The real objectivity of experience implies that our sensibilities, emotions, etc., are organized in a harmony which goes far towards constituting the delight given by poetry and the other arts (Chapter x).

In analysing the criticisms levelled by Dr Richards against A. C. Bradley's *Poetry for Poetry's Sake*, we found that Bradley was right in affirming a contrast between poetic and ordinary experience. The difference does not merely consist in the greater number of impulses which are active in the former: it is essentially a difference of quality. Nor does the greater number of impulses in the poetic experience connote moral superiority. Poetic experience is one of wide acceptance, which reconciles diverse and opposing elements. Moral experience, on the other hand, may be valuable and formative, not through acceptance, but through rejection and choice (Chapter xi). Bradley was right again, when properly understood, in his view of the connection between poetic and ordinary experience. All that passes from the ordinary world into the world of poetic contemplation suffers a deep change in passing, and the connection, though intimate, may not inaptly be pictured as 'underground' (Chapter xii).

A poet, we suggested, is one who, through the metrical ordering of words, creates a unified contemplative experience, highly objective in character. The poet is not to be pictured as communicating a day to day experience better organized than that of other people. The value of his day to day experience, whatever it be, is non-poetic: as a poet, he replaces it by a different, poetic, experience, created through words. He does not communicate or express an experience that existed before the poem was written: he creates a new experience, not only for others, but also (and primarily) for himself (Chapter XIII). Contemplation is an active as well as a tranquil state. The activity of the mind, as Coleridge recognized, is a living, self-creating process. Coleridge's well-known distinction between imagination and fancy is of value, and has an interesting parallel in M. Bergson. Both these writers suggest a close relation between poetry and reality: but, even if the poetic experience implies a reality beyond itself, the proper concern of poetry is with the experience for its own sake, and not for the sake of anything ulterior.

The claim that poetry can take precedence of religion, the latter having now fallen to the status of mere myth, has no warrant. Dr Richards suggests that poetry, as in Coleridge's use of the Wind Harp image, has a unique power to reconcile doctrines which, as doctrines, appear to be in conflict. We found no such reconciliation in Coleridge, and we came to the conclusion that the hope, entertained by Dr Richards, of a new science of criticism, is founded on a confused and pseudo-mystical reading of experience (Chapter XIV).

But while we must reject extravagant claims, it is true, despite the argument of Mr Belgion to the contrary, that poetry is of value, and high value, for the ordering of our minds (Chapter XV). Poetry—we have said in this final chapter—has secondary effects on thought and behaviour, but these are by-products, since they do not arise from the contemplative experience which is its true end. Contemplation occurs in ordinary life and is a fundamental need, removing us for a while from the tumult of action, to give us powers of insight and control. Experience undergoes a profound change when it passes from action into contemplation; it undergoes a further vital change, when it passes into the contemplative experience of the arts, and it is then twice removed from the world of action. Tragedy, even at the single remove, can give order to emotion, and renew perspective: at the double remove of tragic art it can achieve for us a deeply satisfying harmony.

The contemplative experience of poetry—and not of tragic poetry alone—has a special stability, unity and clarity. It is a world apart, in which we may rest. It is complete in itself and is unlike religious contemplation, which creates the need for action. If only for that reason, it can never satisfy all our spiritual needs. Its rank, without any such claim, is sufficiently exalted.

INDEX

(1) NAMES

Abercrombie, Lascelles, 75

Aiken, Conrad, 24

Aristotle, 139

Bacon, 147

Bartlett, E. M., xi, 95

Belgion, Montgomery, Chapter xiv *passim*, 156

Bergson, xi, 25, 30, 51, 121f., 131f., 156

Bradley, A. C., Chapters xi and xii *passim*, 155

Bunyan, 101, 102

Carter, Samuel, 78

Clutton-Brock, A., 64

Coleridge, 25, 28, 101, 105, Chapter xiv *passim*, 156

Dante, 101, 103

Daumier, 94

Donne, 48, 63

Dowson, 55, 59, 61, 64

Driesch, 28

Eliot, 5, 85, 105, 115, 145, 153, 154

Field, Joanna, xi, 71, 151

Gregory, Sir R., 84f.

Hardy, 55, 111

Hartley, 120

H. D., 117

Herbert, George, 152

Herrick, 2, 3, 103

Hoare, Sarah, 85

Horace, 96

Hume, 120

James, William, 94

Joyce, James, 145

Keats, 46, 104

Landor, 2, 3

Lawrence, D. H., 145

Locke, 120

Marvell, 64

Mauron, Charles, x, 69, 78, 83

McDougall, 18

Meredith, 47

Meynell, Alice, 48, 105

Moore, G. E., 11, 29f.

Moore, Sturge, x, 11, 33, 36, 110

Patmore, 59, 61

Plotinus, 121

Poe, 59, 60

Proust, 26, 27

Quiller-Couch, 61

Ravaisson, 121

Richards, I. A., Introduction, 5, 10, 11, Chapter III *passim*, 22, Chapter VII *passim*, 59f., 66, Chapters XI and XII *passim*, 113f., 124f., 138, 149, 155, 156
Roberts, Michael, ix, 149, 150, 152, 153
Ross, W. D., 81, 82
Rossetti, D. G., 31, 40, 63
Russell, Bertrand, 72

Santayana, 82, 83, 154
Schelling, 121, 127
Shelley, 104, 105
Sidgwick, Henry, 33

Smart, Christopher, 85
Stocks, J. L., x
Symons, Arthur, 58, 59
Symons, A. J. A., 79

Thompson, Francis, 40, 47, 69, 135, 140
Tyndall, 18

Van Gogh, 71
Vaughan, 104

Wordsworth, 110, 119, 127

Yeats, 61, 62, 147
Younghusband, Sir F., 84f.

(2) SUBJECTS

Adjustment to life, 10, 11, 19
Adjustment to poetry, 4, 5, 73, 105
Aesthete, 70
Aesthetic attitude, Chapter IX *passim*, 154
Aesthetic emotion, 68, 140
Aesthetic faculty, 68
Aesthetic interest, 37, 38f., 77, *and see* Aesthetic attitude
Aesthetic object, 34, 36, 38f., 54, 57, 81f.
Appreciation, 5, 6, 57, 62, 105
'Art for art's sake', 79
Art, graphic, 38f., 110
Artist, definition of, 107
Attention, 69, 73, 75

Beauty, 10, 22, 29, 32f., 48, 49, 72, 74, 81f.

Censorship, 145

Choice, 92f., 131
Christianity, 152, 153
Communication, 16, Chapter XIII *passim*, 155
Consciousness, 12, 13, 17, 19f., 25, 29, 37, 74, 83
Contemplation, *passim*, especially Chapter IX, 81, 95, 107, 111, 115, 119, 141, Chapter XVI
Creation of experience, 6, 8, 69, Chapter XIII *passim*, 141, 148, 155
Criticism, function of, 52f., 57f., 63f., 100, 106, 140f.
Critics, 22, 53, 57f., 67

Durée, la (vital progression), xi, 39f., 47, 51, 66, 121, 131

Effects of poetry, 5, 6, 98f., 138, 144f., 149

Emotion, 15, 19, 23, 25f., 29, 41, 47, 82, 83, 95f., 119, 122, 132f., Chapter xv *passim*, 146f.
Experience, *see* Chapter headings
  diversity of, 2f., 43, 48, 50, 113
  private, 148

Imagery, 40, Chapter vii *passim*, 62
Imagination and fancy, 119f., 156
Imitation, 138f., 146
Impulses, 11, 13f., 51, 90f., 100, 149
Interpenetration, 24f., 29f., 37, 47, 66, 83
Intuition, self-, 127, 128, 132, 136, 137

Life, poetry and, 6, 8, 69, 70, 83, 86f., 98f., Chapter xvi *passim*

Materialism, 7, 17
Morality, 7, 15, 16, 19, 79f., 93f., 103f., 144f., 151f.
Myth, 124f., 156

Nature, realist and projective doctrines of, 126f.
Nervous activity, 4, 6, 7, 11, Chapter iii *passim*, 91f., 146, 149

Objective theory, 11, 22, Chapter v *passim*

Plasticity of mind, 56, 57, 120
Pleasure, 15, 19, 83
Poet, character of, 16, 69, 70, 94, 102, 115
Poet, definition of, 107
Poetic experience, structure of, 55, 58f., 67, 130
Poetic value, 99f., 108, 117, 139, 142
Practical activity, 5, 6, 71, 77f., 92f., 144f.
Psycho-analysis and art, 69, 109, 149

Reality, 9, 10, 123f., 129, 135, 156
Reasons for admiration, 52f., 67
Religion and poetry, 7, 8, 84f., 103, 104, 125, 150f., 156, 157

Satire, 98, 101, 103, 153
Science, 7, 8, 17
Science and poetry, 84f., 125
Sensuality, 6, 79, 80, 144
Sound in poetry, 32, 58f., 112
Speculative activity, 6, 7, 72, 77, 81, 123, 126f.

Tragedy, 19, 74, 149, 157

Whole and part, 22f., 29f., 37, 38f., 63, 67
Words in poetry, 1, 55, 107f., 139f., 148